NEW SCIENCE
LIBRARY

Lafferty, Peter
   New Science Library / Peter Lafferty; Illustrated by George Fryer.
   p. cm
   Includes index
   Contents : v. 1. Universe and Space -- v. 2. Earth and Its Resources --
v. 3 Living Things -- v.4 Matter and Materials -- v.5. Forces and Energy
-- v.6 Electricity, Magnetism, and Light.
   ISBN 0-89434-160-X (set)
   1. Science--Juvenile literature. 2. Physical sciences--Juvenile literature. [1. Science. 2. Physical sciences.] I. Fryer, George, ill. II. Title.
Q126.4.L34 1996
500--dc20   95-21537
                                                                CIP
                                                                 AC

Printed in the United States of America
X-3

NEW SCIENCE LIBRARY

Universe and Space

Robin Kerrod

Illustrated by George Fryer

Ferguson Publishing Company

Chicago

Contents

Introduction

Every clear night, nature puts on a dazzling show for us. We have only to look upward to the heavens to enjoy it. Thousands upon thousands of stars shine down from an otherwise ink-black sky. When we gaze into this inky blackness, we are looking deep into space, deep into the Universe.

The Earth we live on, the Sun that brings us light and warmth, and the Moon that waxes and wanes as each month goes by – they occupy a tiny corner of the Universe. They are part of the Sun's family, or Solar System. The planets – bodies that circle around the Sun like the Earth does – also belong to this family.

The subject of the photograph here is the most beautiful of the planets, Saturn. It was taken by the space probe Voyager 2. Voyager went on to take close-up pictures of Uranus and Neptune, revealing these far-distant planets clearly for the first time.

The Voyager probe is now moving out of the Solar System toward the stars. It has a very long journey ahead. It is expected to reach the edge of the Solar System early in the 21st century, but it will not get close to another star for at least 40,000 years. This star is one of the nearest to the Solar System that we know.

The most distant stars in the sky are many thousands of times farther away. Yet, as far as the Universe is concerned, these stars are still neighbors. They are part of a family of stars that occupies a great star island, or galaxy, called the Milky Way. The Universe is made up of billions of galaxies, scattered throughout space.

The distances to the farthest galaxies we can detect are unimaginable. They are so far away that their light has taken as long as 12 billion years to reach us. This represents a distance of some 70 billion trillion miles (120 billion trillion kilometers).

In the first half of this volume of the *New Science Library*, we explore the infinite Universe in which we live. We look at the bodies in our celestial backyard and in the remoter regions of space. In the second half, we concentrate on space travel and the human exploration of space. Since Russia's Sputniks pioneered the Space Age in 1957, thousands of satellites have been launched around the Earth and many probes have been dispatched to distant planets. Astronauts now shuttle regularly into orbit; some have remained for more than a year in space stations; and some have even planted their footprints on the Moon. The human race is continuing to push back the boundaries of space, the last great frontier.

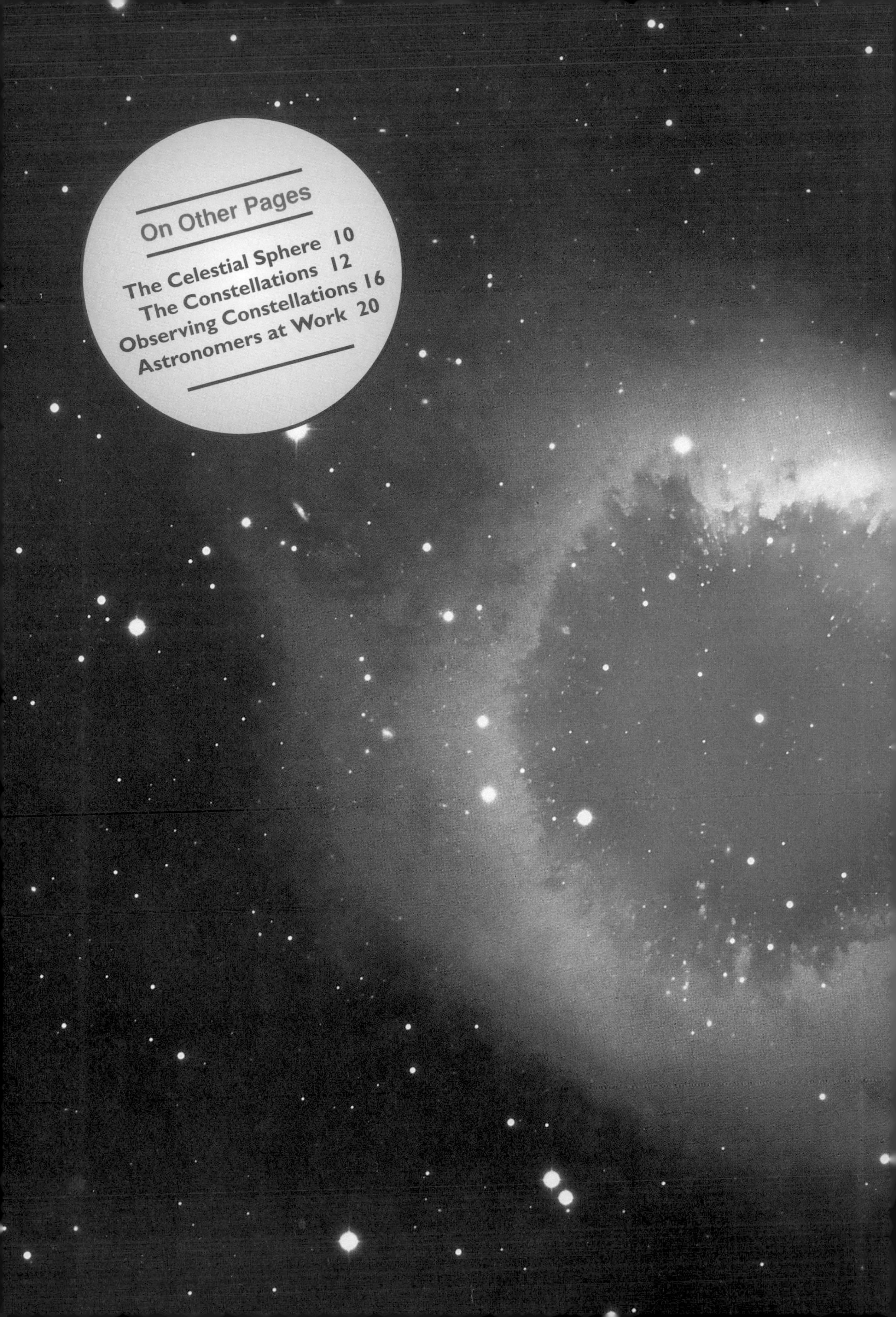

On Other Pages

1 Observing the Heavens

On every clear night, we can see the stars twinkling in the sky, sparkling like jewels on black velvet. Our early ancestors used to do the same, gazing in awe and wonder at what they saw.

People began stargazing seriously when the first civilizations grew up in the Middle East thousands of years ago. They used their observations to work out a calendar, which is a means of dividing up the year into convenient periods. They also looked in the heavens for signs that might mean good luck or bad to their people.

These early stargazers not only looked at the starry heavens, but also tried to explain what they saw there. They noticed how the stars seemed to move across the heavens during the night, rising in the east and setting in the west.

They thought that the stars must therefore be attached to the inside of a huge globe, or sphere, which revolved around the Earth from east to west. We know now, of course, that there is no celestial (heavenly) sphere. The apparent movement of the stars is caused by Earth spinning on its axis once a day.

The early stargazers, then, got it wrong. But with their skillful observations, they laid the foundations of astronomy, the scientific study of the heavens.

The night sky looks beautiful even with the naked eye, but looks magnificent through binoculars or a telescope. The more powerful the telescope, the more stars you can see – millions upon millions of them, as well as other delights, such as this beautiful nebula.

The Celestial Sphere

○ **Why is the idea of a celestial sphere useful?**
○ **Where is the zenith?**
○ **What is the ecliptic?**
○ **Why is Polaris called the Pole Star?**

Ancient stargazers thought the Earth was enclosed by a great celestial sphere that revolved around the Earth once a day. Modern astronomers find the idea of a celestial sphere rotating around the Earth very useful, even though they know it doesn't exist. It provides a convenient way of pinpointing the stars in the heavens.

The diagrams on these pages show various features of the celestial sphere. The sphere appears to spin around on an axis that passes through the north and south celestial poles. The north celestial pole is located directly above the Earth's North Pole, and the south celestial pole is located directly above the Earth's South Pole.

When you are observing the stars, you call the point on the celestial sphere directly over your head the zenith. Your view of the sphere is bounded by your horizon.

The celestial equator

Halfway between the northern and southern celestial poles is the celestial equator. This lies directly above the Earth's Equator. The celestial equator divides the celestial sphere into two hemispheres (half spheres): the northern hemisphere and the southern hemisphere.

The Sun appears to travel around the celestial sphere each year. We call its path the ecliptic. The ecliptic crosses over the celestial equator at two points, always on the same days of the year, on March 21 and September 23.

On these dates, the length of the day is equal to the length of the night all over the world. That is why these dates are called the equinoxes (meaning "equal nights").

celestial north pole

celestial equator

celestial south pole

Star positions

Equinoxes are reference points for the method used to measure the positions of stars in the sky. An astronomer describes the position of a star in the sky in much the same way as a mapmaker describes the position of places on Earth.

A mapmaker uses a system of latitude and longitude. Latitude is the distance a place is north or south of the Equator. Longitude is the distance along the Equator from a certain point. The distances are measured as angles.

An astronomer uses a similar system. A star's latitude, called its declination, is the distance a star is north or south of the celestial equator. It is also expressed as an angle. A star's longitude, called its right ascension, is the distance the star is along the celestial equator, measured from the spring equinox. The right ascension of a star is most commonly measured not in degrees but in hours and minutes.

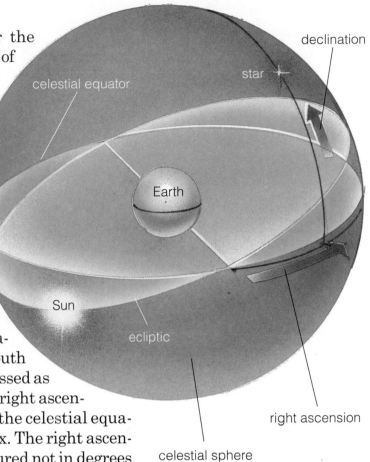

Activity Box

Watch the wheeling

You can easily take photographs to show how the stars seem to wheel around. You need a camera with a time setting and a cable release, a tripod, and a dark sky.

Mount the camera with the lens tilted upward and facing north. Use the cable shutter release to avoid shaking the camera. Leave the shutter open for an hour or longer.

You should end up with a picture like this one, with stars making circular trails. The star at the center that has hardly moved is Polaris. It is also called the Pole Star or North Star, because it lies very close to the north celestial pole.

The Constellations

At first glance, the thousands of stars we see in the night sky appear to be dotted about at random. When you look a little longer, you can see that some stars are brighter than others.

With a little imagination, you can link the bright stars into patterns, which we call the constellations. You can find these star patterns in every part of the sky, and they provide a useful means of finding your way around the heavens.

Ancient constellations

If you look at the same constellations night after night and even year after year, you see that they stay exactly the same. In fact, stargazers in ancient Greece 2,000 years ago saw much the same patterns as we do today.

Those ancient stargazers named the constellations after animals, people, and everyday objects they thought the star patterns looked like. Here they could see a swan, there a bear, a lion, a cup, a man, a woman.

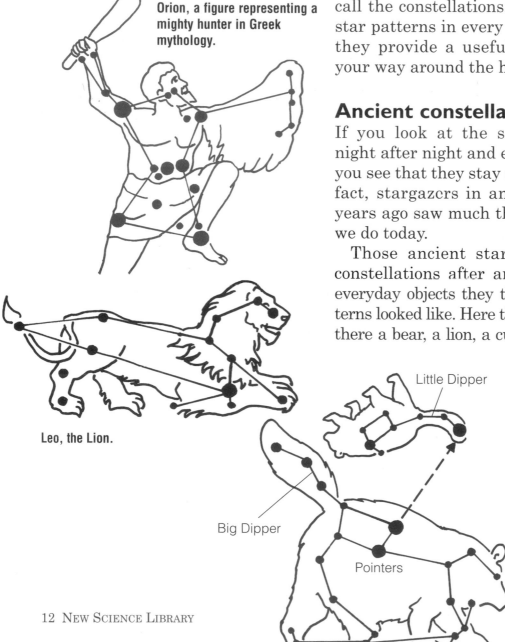

Orion, a figure representing a mighty hunter in Greek mythology.

Leo, the Lion.

Little Dipper

Big Dipper

Pointers

Two familiar constellations in the northern sky, the Big and Little Dippers. They form parts of the constellations of the Great Bear and the Little Bear. Two stars in the Big Dipper point to Polaris, the Pole Star. They are called the Pointers.

Scorpius, the Scorpion.

They made up myths, or stories about how these figures came to be in the heavens.

We still name the constellations after the figures the ancients thought they could see: the Swan, the Great Bear, and the Lion, for example. Astronomers, however, refer to the constellations by their Latin names. For example, the Swan is Cygnus, the Great Bear is Ursa Major, and the Lion is Leo. Astronomers recognize 88 constellations in all (see the table on page 15).

Astrology

Ancient peoples were very superstitious and believed in magic. They thought that what happened in the heavens affected the lives of people on Earth. This belief grew into the study we call astrology.

Many people still believe in astrology. This explains why many newspapers and magazines carry features about what the future holds for people born at different times of the year under different star signs, or signs of the zodiac.

From the Earth, the Sun appears to travel through 12 constellations during the year. They occupy a circle in the heavens called the zodiac. The constellations of the zodiac are the star signs used in astrology.

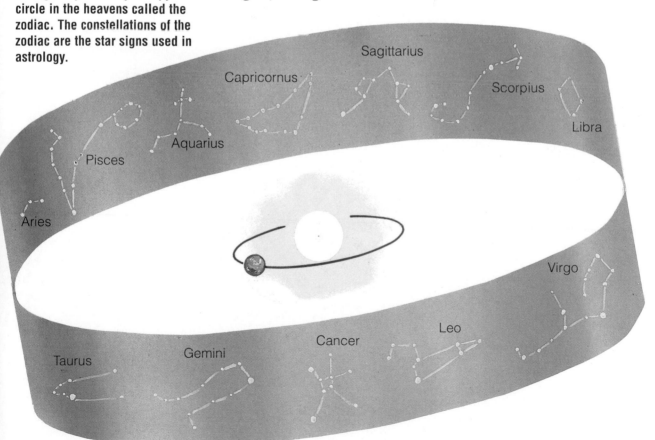

Sagittarius

Capricornus

Scorpius

Libra

Aquarius

Pisces

Aries

Virgo

Taurus

Gemini

Cancer

Leo

Northern and Southern Stars

Stargazers in different parts of the world see different constellations. For example, on the same night,
someone living in Boston, Massachusetts, will see
very different stars from someone else living in
Punta Arenas, Chile, at the southern tip of South
America.

People in different places see different constellations
because the Earth is round. They can see only the stars
that are above the horizon at any time in their part of
the world.

The star maps on these pages show the
main constellations of the northern and southern celestial
hemispheres, the northern
and southern halves of
the celestial sphere.
Stargazers living in
the Earth's north-
ern hemisphere
will be able to see
all the constella-
tions of the
northern celes-
tial hemisphere
at some time
during the year.
They will also be
able to see some
of the constella-
tions of the southern
celestial hemisphere.
Stargazers in the south-
ern hemisphere will be able
to see all the constellations of

| All Seeing |
| People stargazing on the Equator should be able to see all the constellations at some time during the year. |

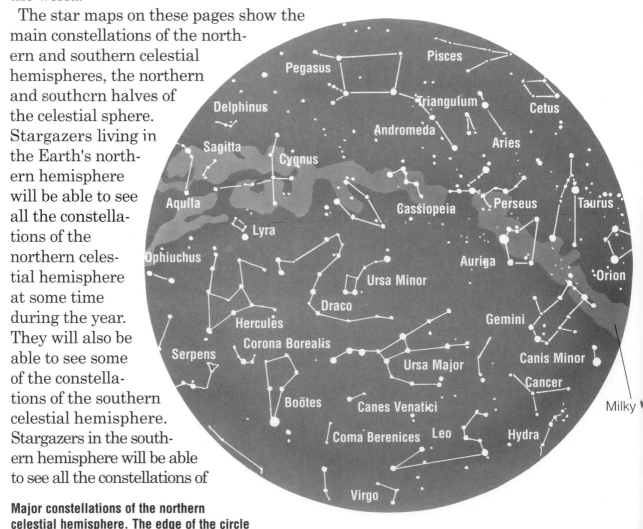

Major constellations of the northern
celestial hemisphere. The edge of the circle
marks the position of the celestial equator.

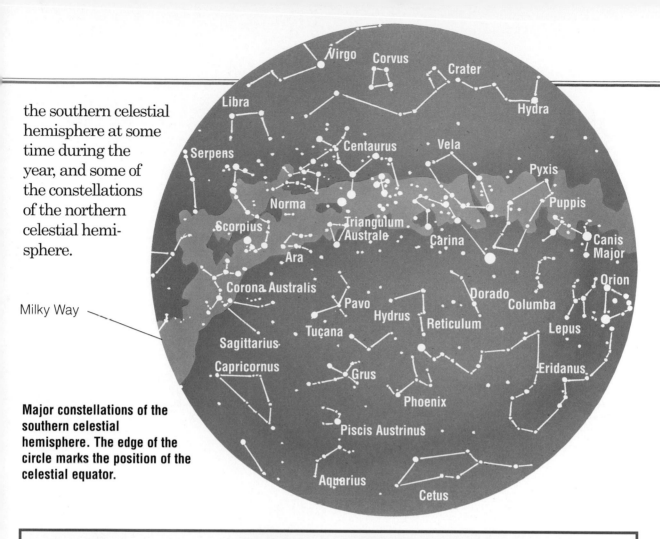

the southern celestial hemisphere at some time during the year, and some of the constellations of the northern celestial hemisphere.

Milky Way

Major constellations of the southern celestial hemisphere. The edge of the circle marks the position of the celestial equator.

Naming the Constellations

Andromeda
Antlia, Air Pump
Apus, Bird of Paradise
Aquarius, Water-Bearer
Aquila, Eagle
Ara, Altar
Aries, Ram
Auriga, Charioteer
Boötes, Herdsman
Caelum, Chisel
Camelopardalis, Giraffe
Cancer, Crab
Canes Venatici, Hunting Dogs
Canis Major, Great Dog
Canis Minor, Little Dog
Capricornus, Sea Goat
Carina, Keel
Cassiopeia
Centaurus, Centaur
Cepheus
Cetus, Whale
Chamaeleon, Chameleon
Circinus, Compasses
Columba, Dove
Coma Berenices, Berenice's Hair
Corona Australis, Southern Crown
Corona Borealis, Northern Crown
Corvus, Crow
Crater, Cup
Crux, Southern Cross

Cygnus, Swan
Delphinus, Dolphin
Dorado, Swordfish
Draco, Dragon
Equuleus, Foal
Eridanus
Fornax, Furnace
Gemini, Twins
Grus, Crane
Hercules
Horologium, Clock
Hydra, Water Snake
Hydrus, Little Snake
Indus, Indian
Lacerta, Lizard
Leo, Lion
Leo Minor, Little Lion
Lepus, Hare
Libra, Scales
Lupus, Wolf
Lynx, Lynx
Lyra, Lyre
Mensa, Table
Microscopium, Microscope
Monoceros, Unicorn
Musca, Fly
Norma, Rule
Octans, Octant
Ophiuchus, SerpentBearer
Orion

Pavo, Peacock
Pegasus, Flying Horse
Perseus
Phoenix, Phoenix
Pictor, Painter
Pisces, Fishes
Piscis Austrinus, Southern Fish
Puppis, Poop (stern of a ship)
Pyxis, Compass
Reticulum, Net
Sagitta, Arrow
Sagittarius, Archer
Scorpius, Scorpion
Sculptor, Sculptor
Scutum, Shield
Serpens, Serpent
Sextans, Sextant
Taurus, Bull
Telescopium, Telescope
Triangulum, Triangle
Triangulum Australe, Southern Triangle
Tucana, Toucan
Ursa Major, Great Bear
Ursa Minor, Little Bear
Vela, Sails
Virgo, Virgin
Volans, Flying Fish
Vulpecula, Fox

Observing Constellations

During the year, the Earth travels in a complete circle in space around the Sun. Therefore, our view of the heavens looking out from the night side of the Earth changes all the time.

You can follow these changes in the night sky yourself by regular observations, say, once a month. To do so, you need to live in, or travel to, a place where the sky is dark enough to see the stars clearly. In most city areas, stars are difficult to see because the whole sky is aglow with light from things like street lamps and advertising signs.

To see how the constellations change, look at the same part of the sky at the same time on the same day of the month. If you can, find a spot where you can look both to the north and to the south. Make sketches of the sky, showing the positions of the constellations, looking north and looking south.

Below: **Looking north at about 10:30 p.m. in mid-January. As on all the north-looking maps, Polaris the Pole Star lies straight ahead. The Square of Pegasus appears low in the west. The handle of the Big Dipper is nearly vertical.**

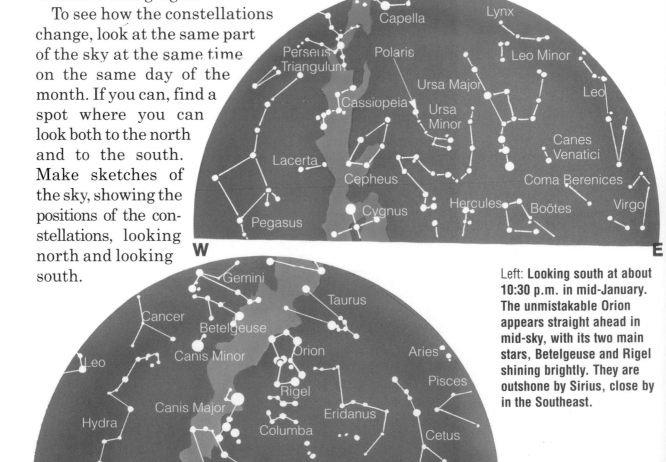

Left: **Looking south at about 10:30 p.m. in mid-January. The unmistakable Orion appears straight ahead in mid-sky, with its two main stars, Betelgeuse and Rigel shining brightly. They are outshone by Sirius, close by in the Southeast.**

While you are observing, keep your eyes open for other astronomical happenings. You are almost certain to spot some meteors streaking across the sky (see page 62). You may even be lucky enough to see a comet (see page 64).

Star maps

Over the next few pages, we show maps of the northern and southern skies for certain months in winter, spring, summer, and fall. They show the main constellations that can be seen over much of North America during these months.

The maps show the constellations in roughly the positions they would appear at about 10:30 at night on the days mentioned. At different times and on different days the constellations will appear in different positions because of the movement of the Earth.

Exactly which constellations you will be able to see depends on where you live. It depends on your latitude, or how far away from the Equator you are. Looking south, for example, stargazers in Florida will be able to see more of the constellations of the southern celestial hemisphere than stargazers farther north.

Below: **Looking north at about 10:30 p.m. in mid-March. The Big Dipper is high in the sky. The W-shape of Cassiopeia appears low down. Two stars are particularly bright: Capella in the mid-sky toward the west and Vega low down toward the east.**

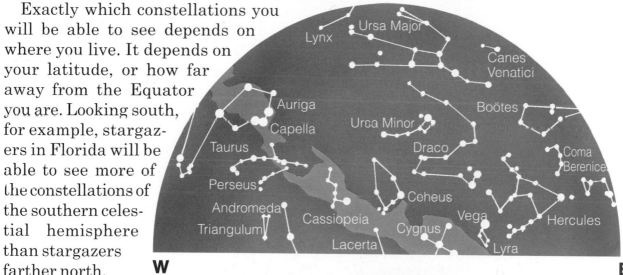

Right: **Looking south at about 10:30 p.m. in mid-March. Orion is close to setting in the west. Sirius, the brightest star in the heavens, still shines brightly. Straight ahead is Leo, easily recognized by the sickle-shaped pattern of stars marking the Lion's head and mane.**

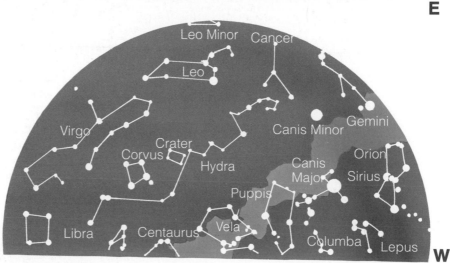

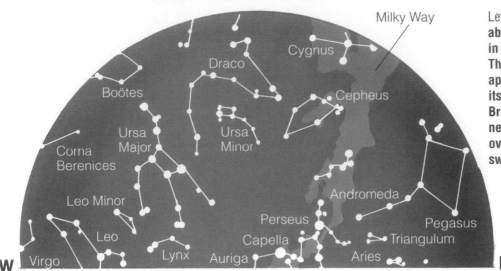

Milky Way

Cygnus
Draco
Boötes
Cepheus
Ursa Major
Ursa Minor
Corna Berenices
Andromeda
Leo Minor
Perseus
Pegasus
Leo
Capella
Triangulum
Virgo
Lynx
Auriga
Aries

W
E

Left: **Looking north at about 10:30 p.m. in mid-July. The Big Dipper now appears toward the west, its handle nearly vertical. Bright Capella is low down near the horizon, while overhead is the beautiful swan shape of Cygnus.**

Right: **Looking south at about 10:30 p.m. in mid-July. Cygnus and Lyra lie overhead. Their brightest stars, Deneb (Cygnus) and Vega (Lyra), form a prominent triangle with Aquila's brightest star, Altair. It is called the Summer Triangle.**

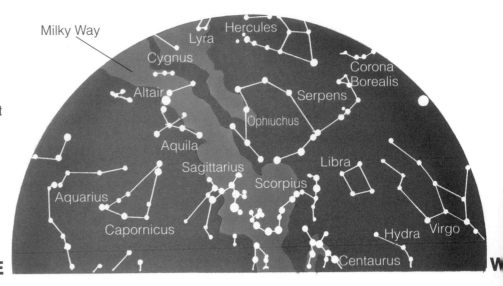

Milky Way

Hercules
Lyra
Cygnus
Corona Borealis
Altair
Serpens
Ophiuchus
Aquila
Libra
Sagittarius
Scorpius
Aquarius
Capornicus
Hydra
Virgo
Centaurus

E
W

Milky Way

Cygnus
Lyra
Vega
Cepheus
Andromeda
Draco
Triangulum
Ursa Minor
Perseus
Hercules
Capella
Camelopardalis
Auriga
Ursa Major
Serpens
Boötes
Orion

W
E

Left: **Looking north at about 10:30 p.m. in mid-September. The handles of the Big and Little Dippers are now nearly horizontal. Capella is bright toward the east. Farther east, Taurus and the Pleiades have come into view.**

Right: **Looking south at about 10:30 p.m. in mid-September. The square of Pegasus has appeared on the scene, heralding the arrival of the fall. Altair toward the west and Fomalhaut lower in the south are the only really bright stars.**

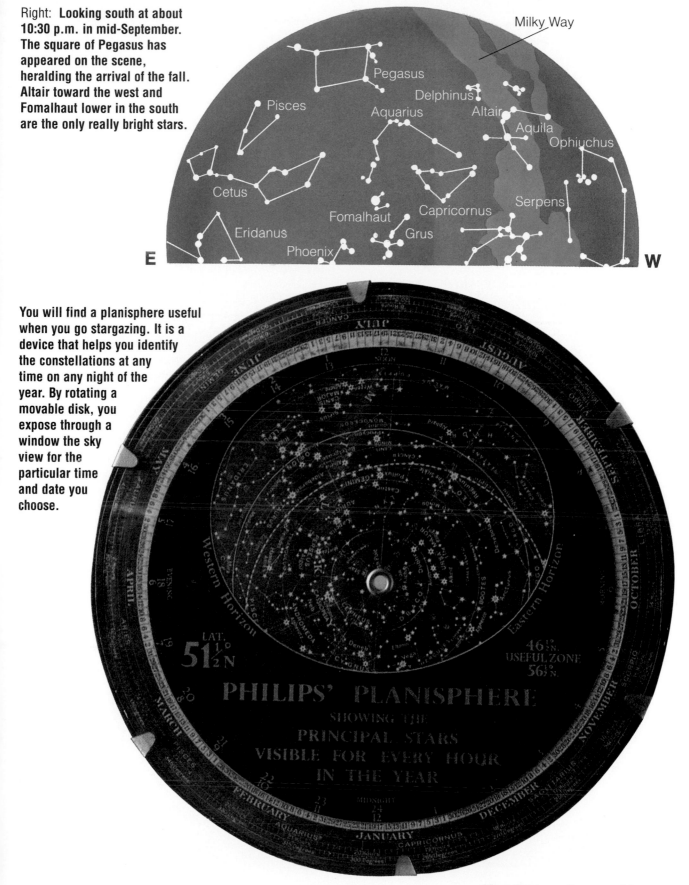

You will find a planisphere useful when you go stargazing. It is a device that helps you identify the constellations at any time on any night of the year. By rotating a movable disk, you expose through a window the sky view for the particular time and date you choose.

Astronomers at Work

Most astronomers begin work when other people are getting ready for bed. Professional astronomers work at observatories, equipped with a variety of instruments they use to study the stars and the other heavenly bodies.

The most important instrument astronomers use is the telescope, a word meaning *seeing far*. A telescope gathers and focuses the light coming from the stars. Other instruments, such as the spectroscope (see

○ What is an observatory?
○ What kinds of telescopes do astronomers use?
○ What are spectral lines?
○ Why do astronomers find photographic film so useful?
○ What is radio astronomy?

Domes at the Kitt Peak National Observatory near Tucson, Arizona. The largest one houses the largest instrument on site, the Mayall telescope. The observatory is located on a peak nearly 6,900 feet (2,100 meters) high.

The Mayall reflector at Kitt Peak Observatory. It has a light-gathering mirror 157 inches (4 meters) across. Like all modern telescopes, it is controlled by computer.

page 22), are then used to analyze the light.

The light reaching us from the stars has traveled for many billions of miles and so is very feeble. Astronomers therefore build large telescopes to collect as much of the light as possible. These instruments are housed inside large domed buildings, which are the most prominent features of most observatories.

Ideally, an observatory should be located on a high peak in a region with a dry climate. There it will command a clearer view of the heavens because it will be above the densest, dustiest, and dampest part of the atmosphere. Major observatories in the United States have locations like this, including Mt. Palomar Observatory near Los Angeles and Kitt Peak Observatory near Tucson, Arizona.

Refractors and reflectors

The Italian scientist Galileo built the first practical telescope nearly 400 years ago. He made it using glass lenses to gather and focus the light. He pioneered modern observational astronomy when he trained his telescope on the heavens in the winter of 1609–1610.

Many astronomers still use lens-type telescopes, or refractors, today, but most use telescopes that have curved mirrors to gather and focus starlight. These telescopes are called reflectors. Isaac Newton built the first reflector around 1668.

Reflectors of Newton's design, known as Newtonians, are popular among amateur astronomers today. Their curved primary (main) mirror gathers light and reflects it back up the telescope tube to a flat second mirror. This, in turn, reflects the light into a viewing eyepiece.

Distant Candles

The world's biggest telescopes are so light-sensitive that they could detect the light from a single candle over a distance of 15,000 miles (25,000 km).

Telescope Cameras

Astronomers at large observatories do not often look through their telescopes. Instead, they use them as giant cameras and take pictures of the heavens on photographic film.

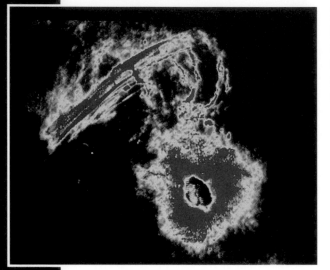

Radio pictures of the heavens are made using computers. This image shows powerful radio signals coming from the center of our Galaxy.

Above: **You can split a beam of Sunlight into a spectrum by passing it through a prism of glass. The different colors represent the different wavelengths that combine to make white light.**

The reason for doing this is that film is more sensitive to light than the human eye. The longer you expose film, the more light it collects. Long-exposure photographs taken through telescopes can therefore show stars very much fainter than the human eye can see.

To record the faintest stars, exposures of several hours are necessary. During this time, the telescopes must move to follow the stars as they appear to wheel across the sky.

Analyzing the light

Astronomers can find out an amazing amount of information about a distant star from its faint light. First they have to split up the light into a spectrum, or spread of different colors like those in a rainbow. To do this, they use an instrument called a spectroscope.

They find that the spectrum of a star is crossed by numbers of dark lines, called spectral lines. From the overall appearance of the spectrum and the positions of the lines in it, astronomers can determine what the star is like. They can tell its temperature, its composition, whether it is moving toward or away from us, and many other things about it.

Tuning in to the heavens

Stars give out not only light rays, but also radiation of all kinds, including X-rays, infrared rays, and radio waves. The atmosphere absorbs most kinds of radiation, but lets through light. It also lets through radio waves. This has led to a branch of study called radio astronomy. Astronomers can also study all kinds of radiation from the stars by sending instruments into space on satellites (see page 100).

Above: **Some of the dishes of the Very Large Array radio telescope near Socorro, New Mexico. There are 27 dishes in all, which can be moved and arranged in different ways to tune in to heavenly radio waves.**

A Bell Telephone engineer named Karl Jansky pioneered radio astronomy in 1931 while investigating radio interference. He discovered that some interference came from outer space. Six years later, the U.S. scientist Grote Reber built the world's first radio telescope and began scanning the heavens for radio signals. Reber's telescope consisted of a metal dish about 30 feet (9 meters) across. The dish picked up radio signals and focused them onto an antenna in the center. The signals were then fed to a sensitive radio receiver.

Most modern radio telescopes are of similar design, but are very much bigger. The world's biggest radio dish is located at Arecibo, Puerto Rico. It measures 1,000 feet (305 meters) across. It is built into the top of a mountain (see page 123).

Right: **This radio telescope in New South Wales, Australia, has a dish 210 feet (64 meters) across.**

2 Stars, Galaxies, and the Universe

W hen we gaze into the dark night sky, we are looking into the depths of space. We can see thousands upon thousands of stars dotted about in all directions. They form part of our great star island, or Galaxy, the Milky Way. In powerful telescopes we can see thousands and thousands of other galaxies. Stars, galaxies, and space make up the Universe. Thanks to astronomers ancient and modern, we have a good idea of what the Universe is like. The stars are great globes of searing hot gas that shine for billions of years before they die, often in a spectacular explosion. The galaxies each contain hundreds of billions of stars, and the Universe contains hundreds of billions of galaxies, all rushing headlong away from one another.

We know that the Universe is bigger than we can ever imagine. It is so big that it would take a beam of light more than 15 billion years to reach what we think might be the edge of the Universe.

How did the Universe begin? Has it always been like it is now? What will happen to it in the future? These are questions that philosophers, religious people, and astronomers have been disussing for centuries. The branch of astronomy concerned with the origins and evolution of the Universe is called cosmology. As we shall see later, astronomers believe they know how and when the Universe began. They are not so sure about how or when it will end.

A view of the heavens in the constellation Sagittarius. The cloud of glowing gas in the center is the famous Trifid Nebula. Bright, colorful clouds like this are dotted around the Milky Way Galaxy, the great star island to which our Sun belongs.

What Stars Are Like

○ How far away are the stars?
○ How big are stars?
○ What is a star's magnitude?
○ How do stars produce their energy?
○ What is a pulsar?
○ What is the main feature of a black hole?

The stars we see in the night sky lie very far away from us, yet we know a lot about them. One reason is that we have been able to study one star very closely, the star we call the Sun. The Sun lies only about 93 million miles (150 million km) away.

The next nearest star, however, lies over 25 million million miles away. It is called Proxima Centauri in the constellation Centaurus. It lies so far away that its light, traveling at 186,000 miles (300,000 km) a second, takes over four years to reach us. Therefore we say it lies over four light-years away.

Astronomers often express distances in space in terms of light-years. Only a few stars lie closer than 10 light-years away. Many stars lie thousands of light-years away.

Moving stars

The stars seem to be fixed in position in the sky, but they are actually hurtling through space. The reason we don't see them move is that they lie so very

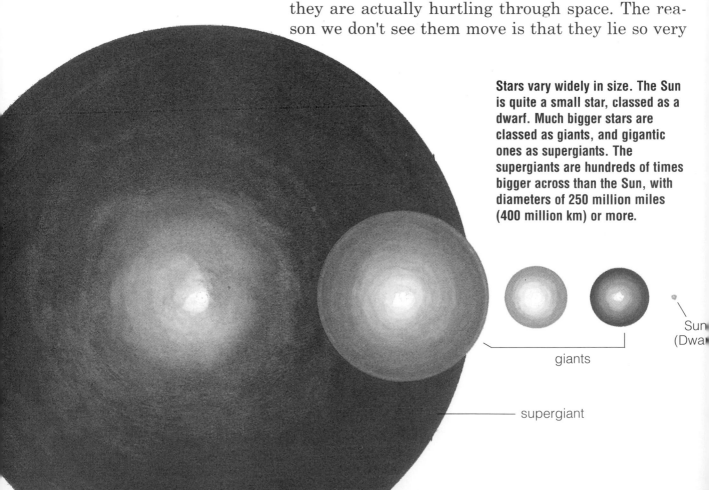

Stars vary widely in size. The Sun is quite a small star, classed as a dwarf. Much bigger stars are classed as giants, and gigantic ones as supergiants. The supergiants are hundreds of times bigger across than the Sun, with diameters of 250 million miles (400 million km) or more.

giants

Sun (Dwar

supergiant

far away. In fact, we can see a few of the nearest stars moving. They change their position slightly year by year. Barnard's Star shows the biggest change – a few thousandths of a degree a year.

Star brightness

We measure a star's brightness in units of magnitude, following a system devised by ancient Greek astronomers. They graded the stars visible to the naked eye into six categories of brightness, or magnitudes. The brightest were 1st magnitude, the next brightest were 2nd magnitude, and the faintest were 6th magnitude.

Astronomers have extended the magnitude scale beyond 1 to negative values to describe the brightness of very bright stars like Sirius (magnitude –1.4), the brighest star in the sky.

They have also extended the scale in the other direction to describe the brightness of faint stars we can't see with the naked eye, such as Proxima Centauri (magnitude 11).

The Nearest Stars		
Star	**Constellation**	**Distance (light-years)**
Prox. Centauri	Centaurus	4.3
Alpha Centauri	Centaurus	4.3
Barnard's Star	Ophiuchus	5.8
Wolf 359	Leo	7.6
Lalande 21185	Ursa Major	8.1
Sirius	Canis Major	8.7
UV Ceti	Cetus	8.9
Ross 154	Sagittarius	9.5
Ross 248	Andromeda	10.3
Eta Eridani	Eridanus	10.7

The Brightest Stars		
Star	**Constellation**	**Apparent magnitude**
Sirius	Canis Major	–1.4
Canopus	Carina	–0.7
Alpha Centauri	Centaurus	–0.2
Arcturus	Boötes	0.0
Vega	Lyra	0.0
Capella	Auriga	0.1
Rigel	Orion	0.1
Procyon	Canis Minor	0.4
Achernar	Eridanus	0.5
Beta Centauri	Centaurus	0.6

True Brightness

The brightness of a star we see from Earth is only an apparent brightness. It does not describe the true brightness of the star. This is because the stars all lie at different distances from us. To compare their true brightness, we must look at them from the same distance. Astronomers have chosen a distance of 33 light-years. We call the brightness of a star at this distance its absolute magnitude.

Inside the stars

Stars are great globes of very hot gases. The main gases are hydrogen and helium. Stars use the hydrogen as fuel in the reactions (processes) that produce the energy they need to keep shining.

These reactions take place in the heart of a star, where the temperature is tens of millions of degrees. They are nuclear reactions, which involve the nuclei (centers) of atoms. What happens is that the nuclei of atoms of hydrogen fuse (join) together, forming nuclei of helium atoms. In this nuclear fusion process fantastic amounts of energy are given out. This energy eventually makes its way to the surface of the star, from where it pours into space as light, heat, and other radiation.

The temperature at the surface of a star varies widely. The yellowish-colored Sun has a surface tem-

The apparent brightness of a star does not tell us how bright the star really is. A truly dim star that is closer to us might appear much brighter than a truly bright star that is much farther away.

3. 4.

1.

2.

perature of about 10,000°F (5,500°C). Bright blue-white stars can be four or five times hotter. On the other hand, reddish stars may have a temperature of less than 5,500°F (3,000°C).

Life and death of a star

Stars have so much hydrogen fuel for their nuclear furnace that they may shine for billions of years. Our Sun, for example, has been shining for five billion years and should continue to shine for another five billion years. Then it will run out of nuclear fuel, and start to die. All the stars will die one day.

The illustration below shows typical stages in the life-cycle of stars. Not all stars go through the complete cycle. Stars like the Sun, for example, swell up into a red giant, then shrink again into a tiny dense body called a white dwarf.

Much more massive stars go the whole way, eventually blasting themselves apart in a supernova explosion. The matter that remains shrinks to form a very dense body called a neutron star, or pulsar. It rotates rapidly and sends out energy in rhythmic pulses. It is so dense that just a teaspoonful of it would weigh millions of tons. The biggest stars shrink almost to nothing, creating the most fearsome body in the Universe, a black hole.

7.

6.

5.

Stages in the life of a star:

1. The star is born in a cloud of gas and dust, or nebula.
2. The cloud shrinks to form a globe.
3. The globe starts to shine as a star when nuclear processes begin inside it.
4. The star shines steadily for most of its life.
5. The star swells up into a red giant.
6. The star continues to expand into a supergiant.
7. The supergiant is unstable and eventually explodes as a supernova.

The Big Attraction

A black hole is a region of space with enormous gravity. Nothing can escape from it, not even light. That is how it gets its name.

Star Companions

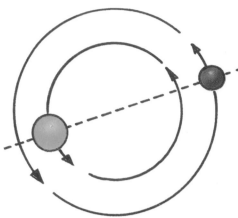

The two stars in a binary system circle around an imaginary point in space. It marks the center of mass of the system.

Below: **This glowing wisp of gas in the constellation Cygnus is what remains of a supernova explosion that took place tens of thousands of years ago.**

Our star, the Sun, travels through space by itself, but many stars travel along with other stars as companions. In fact, only about a third of all stars travel by themselves. Most stars have a single companion. We call such pairs double stars. If you look carefully at Mizar, the middle star in the handle of the Big Dipper, you can see another star close by, named Alcor. We call such a pair a naked-eye double or an optical pair. You can see many more double stars when you look through binoculars or a telescope.

Many stars appear to be doubles only because they happen to lie in the same direction in space. Some stars are true doubles, traveling through space together. We call them binary stars.

In a binary system, the two stars circle around each other. In some binary systems, the stars circle in the same plane as we are viewing them (see diagram at left). At regular intervals, each star passes in front of the other. When this happens, the brightness of the system drops suddenly. Then the stars

move on, and their full brightness is restored. This kind of star system is called an eclipsing binary. The best known eclipsing binary is the first discovered, Algol, in the constellation Perseus.

Variable stars

Eclipsing binaries form one group of variable stars, stars that vary noticeably in brightness. Other stars are true variables. They are single stars that vary in brightness because of processes going on inside them. The best known group of true variables are the Cepheids. They are named after the first one discovered, the star Delta Cephei in the constellation Cepheus.

New stars

Sometimes what seems to be a new star suddenly appears in the sky. What happens is that an existing faint star suddenly flares up and becomes many thousands of times brighter. We call such a star a nova (plural, novae).

More rarely, a star literally explodes and increases in brightness millions of times. We call it a supernova. Massive stars explode into supernovae at the ends of their lives (see page 29).

Right: **A supernova appears in the outer regions of a distant galaxy, looking like a brilliant new star (circled in red). The pictures show the galaxy as it was before and after the event.**

Clusters and Clouds

○ **What is the best known star cluster?**
○ **Why are globular clusters so called?**
○ **What is a nebula?**
○ **Can you see any nebulae with the naked eye?**

The stars in the constellations stay in the same positions year after year and century after century. They appear to be grouped together in space, but usually they are not. Mostly, they lie at different distances from us. They only appear together because they happen to lie in the same direction in space.

Some stars, however, do form groups and travel through space together. We call these groups clusters. You can see the best known cluster in the constellation Taurus. It is called the Pleiades. It is not far from a bright reddish star called Aldebaran.

In the Pleiades the stars are far apart. It is an example of an open cluster. If you have good eyesight, you might be able to see seven bright stars in the cluster. That is how it gets its other name, the Seven Sisters.

This is the famous Pleiades star cluster, also called the Seven Sisters. All the bright stars in the cluster are young and hot.

Globular clusters

The southern constellation Centaurus contains what appears to be a large bright star called Omega Centauri. If you look at it in a powerful telescope, however, you find that it is actually made up of thousands upon thousands of stars packed tightly together into a globe shape.

Omega Centauri is one of the finest examples of what is called a globular cluster. Like the others, it is made up mostly of old stars. Open clusters, on the other hand, are made up mostly of young stars.

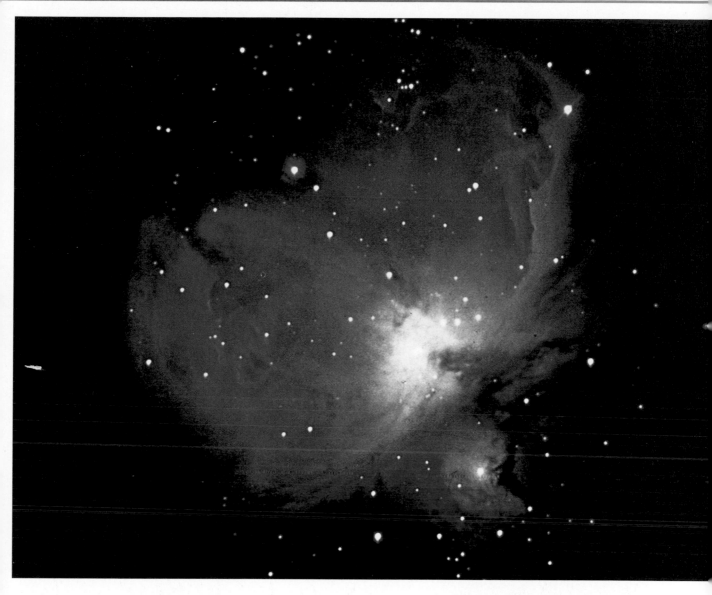

Clouds in the heavens

The space between the stars is not completely empty. It contains traces of gas and scattered particles of solid matter like fine dust. In some places, the gas and dust have come together to form denser cloud-like masses. Astronomers call such a mass a nebula, the Latin word for "cloud."

In some parts of the sky, nearby stars light up the clouds, and we see them as bright nebulae. In other parts, the clouds block the light from distant stars, and we see them as dark nebulae. You can see one bright nebula clearly with the naked eye. You can find it in the constellation Orion beneath the three stars that form Orion's belt.

The Great Nebula in Orion can be seen with the naked eye. You need a telescope, however, to appreciate its great beauty.

The Galaxies

○ **What is the Milky Way?**
○ **Can we see any other galaxies?**
○ **Which is the nearest galaxy?**
○ **Who pioneered study of the galaxies?**
○ **How many galaxies are there?**

On a really dark clear night, the starry heavens are a magnificent sight. If you look carefully, you can see a faint band of light arching across the sky. We call this band the Milky Way. When you look at the Milky Way through binoculars or a telescope, you find that it is made up of thousands and thousands of faint stars.

The Milky Way gives us a clue about how stars are arranged in space. They are grouped into great star islands, or galaxies. Many of these galaxies are shaped like a disk. The stars we see in the night sky all belong to one of these disklike galaxies.

When we look at the Milky Way, we are looking at a slice, or cross section, through the disk of our galaxy. Astronomers call our galaxy the Milky Way, or just the Galaxy.

Spinning spirals

The stars in the Galaxy are not evenly distributed. Some stars group together to form a bulge at the center, or nucleus. Others lie on curved arms that spiral out from the nucleus.

We know of many galaxies like this, which we call spiral galaxies. The Milky Way and all the other galaxies rotate as they travel through space. If they speeded up, they would look like the spinning fireworks we call Catherine wheels.

If we could look at the Galaxy from a distance, it would look much like this. This is another spiral galaxy of a similar type in the constellation Ursa Major.

Stars galore

The Galaxy is bigger than we can ever imagine. It measures some 100,000 light-years across. All of the thousands of stars we see in the night sky belong to the Galaxy. Altogether, it is thought to contain at least 100 billion stars.

Our own star, the Sun, sits on one of the Galaxy's spiral arms. It is quite a way from the center of the Galaxy, about 30,000 light-years. At this distance out, the Sun circles once around the center of the Galaxy every 225 million years.

The Great Nebula

In the constellation of Andromeda you can see a fuzzy patch that looks like a nebula. In fact we call it the Great Nebula in Andromeda.

When you look at it through a powerful telescope, however, you can see that it isn't a nebula at all. It is made up of thousands of stars gathered together into a disk shape. In other words, the Andromeda nebula is another galaxy.

A region of the Milky Way in the constellation Sagittarius. The Milky Way is densest in this constellation because the center of the Galaxy lies in this part of the heavens.

Long Voyage

In orbit, the space shuttle travels at a speed of about 17,500 mph (28,000 km/h). Traveling at this speed, it would take the shuttle more than 4 billion years to journey from one side of our Galaxy to the other. This is nearly as long as the Earth has existed.

The Clouds of Magellan

Amazing Quasars

The word *quasar* is short for quasistellar objects, meaning an object that looks like a star but isn't. Astronomers found the first quasars in 1962. They proved to be very distant, thousands of times smaller than an ordinary galaxy, yet hundreds of time brighter.

There are two other fuzzy patches that look like nebulae in far southern skies. The Portuguese seaman Ferdinand Magellan noticed them on his epic voyage around the world in the 1500s, and they are named after him. They are called the Large and Small Magellanic Clouds and are not nebulae but galaxies.

The Magellanic Clouds are the closest galaxies to our own. The Large Magellanic Cloud is the closer of the two, being about 170,000 light-years away. This is much closer than the Andromeda galaxy, which lies over 2 million llight-years away.

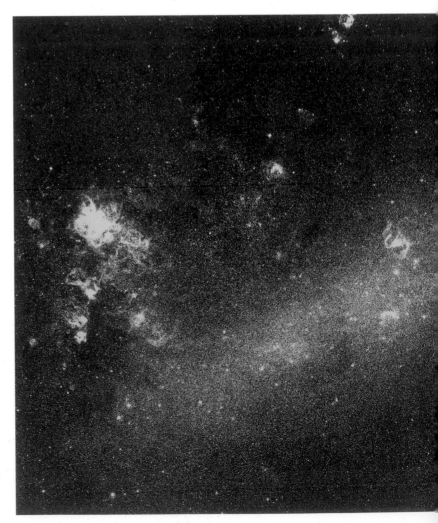

The Large Magellanic Cloud can be seen as a fuzzy patch of light in far southern skies. To the naked eye, it appears bigger and brighter than the Andromeda galaxy, but that is only because it is much closer to us.

Classifying the galaxies

The Andromeda galaxy is a spiral galaxy, much like our own only much bigger. The Magellanic Clouds, on the other hand, have little structure and are classed as irregular galaxies. About 40 percent of all galaxies are spirals or irregular. The rest are round or oval in shape and are known as ellipticals. They are much like spiral galaxies without the arms.

The classification of galaxies into spirals, ellipticals, and irregulars was suggested by the U.S. astronomer Edwin Hubble. He pioneered study of the outer galaxies in the 1920s, working with the 100-inch (25 cm) telescope at Mt. Wilson Observatory near Los Angeles. This was the world's largest telescope at the time.

Another class of galaxies is now recognized, called active galaxies. They are noted for their enormous energy output. Many give out this energy as radio waves and are sometimes called radio galaxies. Astronomers believe that the very bright and very distant bodies called quasars are the centers of highly active galaxies.

The Great Nebula in Andromeda is a neighbor of our own Galaxy, but its light still takes over 2 million years to reach us.

Groups of galaxies

Galaxies tend to group together in space. Our Galaxy, the Andromeda galaxy, and the Magellanic Clouds form part of a small cluster of galaxies known as the Local Group.

All together, the Local Group contains about 30 galaxies. Other clusters are much bigger. One in the constellation Virgo is estimated to contain over 3,000 galaxies.

1.

○ Is the Universe getting bigger?
○ What was the Big Bang?
○ How old is the Universe?
○ Will the Universe ever end?

2.

The Expanding Universe

Astronomers find that the outer galaxies are hurtling away from us at high speed in all directions. It seems as if the whole Universe is expanding, and astronomers think that it is. This means that in the past the Universe was smaller than it is today, and that in the future it will get bigger.

By working backwards, astronomers have estimated that the expansion of the Universe started about 15 billion years ago. In other words, the Universe was born then.

Astronomers believe that the Universe was born in an event they call the Big Bang, which we can think of as a gigantic explosion. The Big Bang created the Universe and set it expanding.

At first the Universe was tiny, super hot, and full of energy in the form of radiation. Just seconds later, it had cooled down enough to allow the basic particles of matter – protons, neutrons, and electrons – to form. These particles did not start to come together to form atoms until hundreds of thousands of years later.

The Big Bang

1. Created the Universe and started it expanding. At first it was unbelievably hot.

2. Gradually it cooled down and matter began to form. In time, great clumps of matter began collecting together into galaxies.

3. After about 15,000 billion years, the Universe became like it is today.

4. Still expanding.

Star formation

No one knows how long it was before this basic atomic matter began forming into stars and galaxies. Probably it happened before the Universe was 2 billion years old, about 13 billion years ago. One reason astronomers think this is because they have detected light from quasars (see page 36) that seems to have been traveling for about 13 billion years.

What happens now?

What will happen to the Universe in the future. Probably it could do one of two things.It could go on expanding for ever until it runs out of energy. Or, it could eventually stop expanding and begin shrinking. Eventually it would shrink into nothing, just as it expanded from nothing. Such an event is termed the Big Crunch. Maybe another Big Bang would follow the Big Crunch to create a new Universe.

Activity Box

Make the Universe expand

All the distant galaxies are rushing headlong away from us, but this doesn't mean that we are at the center of the Universe. All the galaxies, our own included, are rushing away from one another. You can demonstrate this with a balloon.

Partly blow up a balloon and, with a pen, mark dots on it about an inch (2.5 cm) apart. Think of the balloon as the Universe and the dots as galaxies. Now expand the Universe (blow up the balloon) and look what happens to the galaxies (dots). You will notice that they have all moved farther apart from one another.

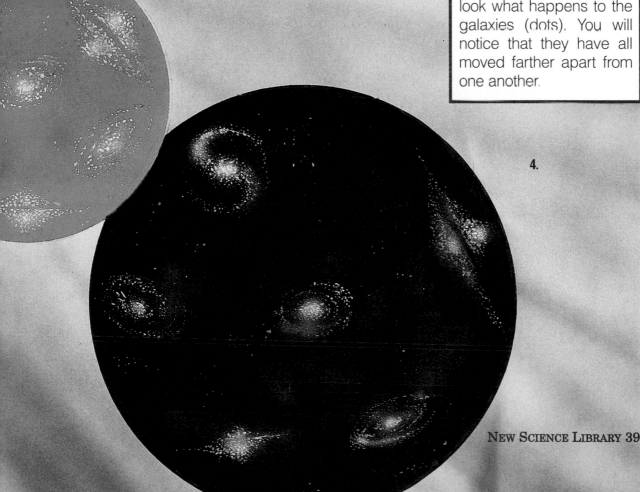

3.

4.

On Other Pages

3 The Sun's Family

Among the countless billions of stars that make up the Universe, one is very important to us. It is the star we know as the Sun.

The Earth circles in space around the Sun every year. It is one of nine large planets, which form the major part of the Sun's family, or Solar System. The word solar comes from the Latin word *sol*, meaning Sun.

Some planets lie closer to the Sun than the Earth; others lie much farther away. Some are much smaller than the Earth; others are much bigger.

The Solar System also includes many other smaller bodies. They include the satellites, or Moons, that circle around many of the planets. The one we know best is the Earth's only satellite, the Moon. It is Earth's closest neighbor in space, and is close enough to visit and explore.

The Moon appears in our skies on most nights. Usually at night we can also see falling stars, which are actually meteors. Occasionally, we can see brilliant comets with long tails that can stretch halfway across the sky. Meteors and comets are among the other bits and pieces that make up the Solar System.

Solar eruptions emit clouds of charged particles capable of disrupting radio transmissions on Earth and sending magnetic navigational systems haywire. A U.S. Navy's research rocket carried the camera that took this picture.

The Solar System

The nine planets travel around the Sun in roughly circular paths, or orbits. If you could look down on the Solar System from a distance, you would see that they all travel counter-clockwise – in the opposite direction to the hands of a clock (see the diagram below).

In order, going away from the Sun, the planets are Mercury, Venus, Earth, Mars, Jupiter, Saturn, Uranus, Neptune, and Pluto. They travel around the Sun at different speeds. Mercury travels fastest, taking just 88 days to circle the Sun. Pluto travels slowest, taking nearly 250 years.

Pluto wanders at times more than 4,500 million miles (7,000 million km) from the Sun, but it is still held in the grip of the Sun's gravity. The Sun has an enormous pull because it is so massive. It has 750 times more mass than all the other bodies in the Solar System put together.

Pluto is usually the most distant planet (see page 79), but it is not the most distant body in the Solar System. Astronomers have recently discovered even smaller bodies farther

This diagram gives an idea of the vast size of the Solar System. It shows the orbits of the nine planets drawn roughly to scale. As you can see, the Earth lies relatively close to the Sun, but it is still about 93 million miles (150 million km) away. The outermost planet, Pluto, lies 40 times farther away!

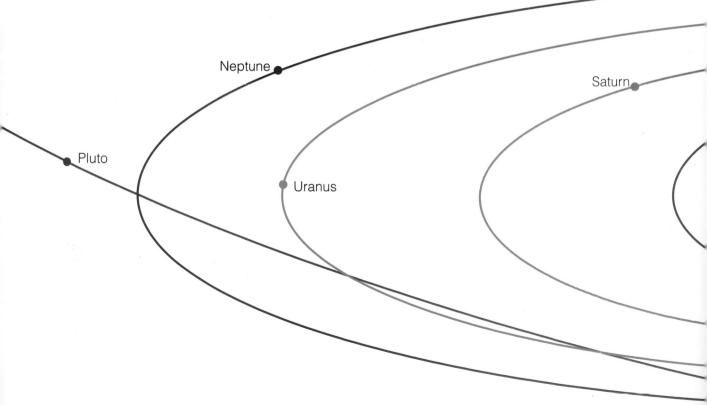

away. They also know that the chunks of icy rock that become comets lie farther out still. They think that a cloud of comets could reach out as far as two light-years (about 12 million million miles or 20 million million km). This is halfway to the nearest stars!

Copernicus's Idea

For thousands of years, everybody believed that the Earth was the center of the Universe. They thought that the Sun, stars, and planets circled around the Earth. Not until the 1500s did someone put forward the idea that the Earth and the planets circle around the Sun. The person who suggested this Sun-centered, or solar, system was Nicolaus Copernicus, a Polish priest and astronomer, who died in 1543.

○ **How big is the Solar System?**
○ **What keeps the Solar System together?**
○ **In which direction do the planets circle the Sun?**
○ **Who first thought of the Solar System?**
○ **How old is the Solar System?**
○ **Are there other solar systems among the stars?**

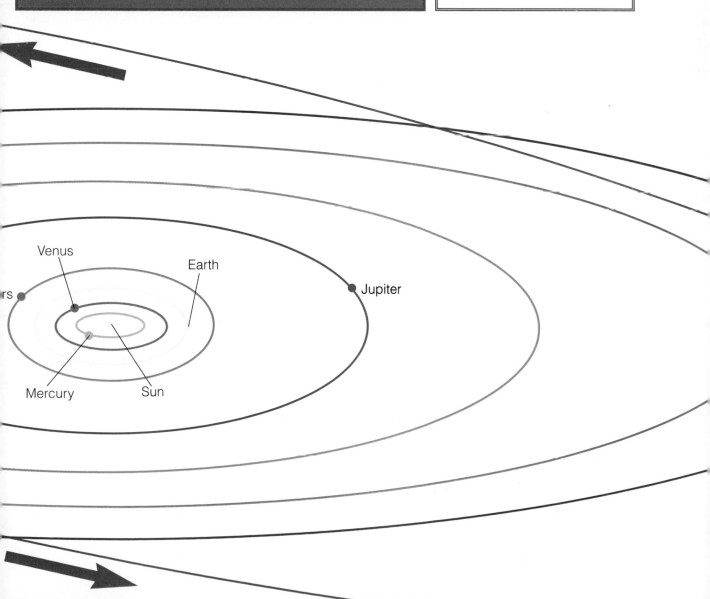

Birth of the Solar System

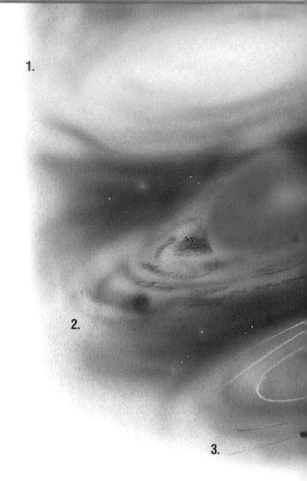

About five billion years ago, the Sun and Solar System did not exist. All that existed in the space they now occupy was a huge cloud of gas and dust. It measured many billions of miles across. There are many such clouds in the Universe. Astronomers call them nebulae (see page 33).

Then, something made the particles of gas and dust in the nebula start to come together under the influence of gravity. Astronomers think that it might have been the shock wave produced when a nearby star exploded.

Denser and hotter

The cloud began shrinking and became denser and denser as the gas and dust came together. It gradually formed into a disk like shape and started to rotate, something like a hurricane. It also became hotter.

Most of the matter collected in a bulge in the center, which in time became globe-shaped. The globe continued to shrink, getting hotter and hotter. It began to glow, orange and then red. Soon the temperature inside the globe rose to tens of millions of degrees. This set off processes (nuclear reactions) that gave out so much energy that the globe began shining as a star – our star, the Sun.

The planets form

It was much cooler in the disk of matter rotating around the newborn Sun. There, matter was coming together to form solid lumps. The lumps became bigger as they bumped into one another, and in time they grew into the planets.

In the future

The Solar System is not going to change much in the near future. This is because the Sun will continue shining as it does today for millions of years more.

A dramatic change will take place in another five billion years' time. This is when the Sun will run out of its nuclear fuel. It will start to swell up into a red giant, so big that it might reach out past the orbit of Venus. The Earth will be scorched to a cinder.

Ussher's Estimate

In the 1600s an Irish archbishop, James Ussher, said that he had worked out from so-called references in the Bible that the Earth was created, exactly as it is now, in 4004 BC.

1. The Solar System was born in a vast cloud of gas and dust.

2. The cloud began to shrink and rotate. In time it formed into a bulging disk.

3. The matter in the disk gradually separated out, with a glowing globe at the center and lumps circling farther out.

4. Eventually, the system became like the Solar System we find today, with a central Sun and orbiting planets.

5. Millions of years in the future, the Sun will expand into a red giant star and could swallow up Mercury and Venus.

4.

5.

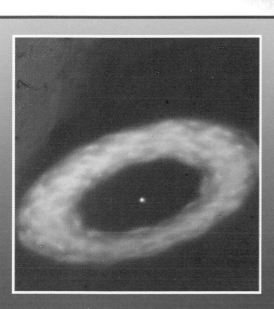

Other Solar Systems

Our Sun is a very ordinary kind of star. We know of many millions of stars like it in our Galaxy alone. If our Sun has planets circling around it, so must many other stars. The space probe IRAS (see page 109) has already spotted disks of matter circling around other stars, such as Vega (left).

If there are other solar systems, are there some planets like Earth, and do any of these Earth-like planets have life on them? We don't know the all answers to these questions – yet.

The Sun

To us on Earth, the Sun is the most important thing there is. It sends us light and heat, making our world a comfortable, bright, and colorful place to live.

Without the Sun, the Earth would be cold and dark. It would also be a dead world, with no plants or animals. Plants need Sunlight to make their food, and animals eat plants or other animals that eat plants.

The Sun doesn't look very big in the sky, but that is only because it lies far away, at an average distance of 93 million miles (150 million km). In fact, compared with the Earth, the Sun is gigantic. It measures 865,000 miles (1,390,000 km) in diameter. It's volume could swallow more than a million Earths.

Our star

The Sun is a very different body from the Earth and the other planets. It is a star, like the other stars in the sky, but very much closer. It is a ball of very hot gas, mainly hydrogen and helium. The temperature at the surface of the Sun is about 10,000°F (5,500° C), but in the center it rises as high as 27,000,000°F

○ **Why is the Sun important to us?**
○ **How big is the Sun?**
○ **What is it made of?**
○ **How hot is it?**
○ **What are Sunspots?**
○ **What is the solar wind?**
○ **What are eclipses?**

Below: **The surface of the Sun is a seething mass of boiling gas. Flames and fountains of glowing gas shoot high above the surface. Streams of electrified particles streak away and disappear into space, forming the so-called solar wind.**

prominences

solar flare

photosphere

Sunspot

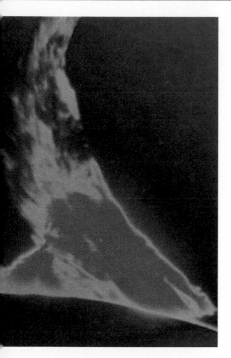

Above: **This is a solar flare, a tongue of flame leaping above the Sun's surface.**

Below: **Space shuttle astronauts took this photograph of the Southern Lights, or the aurora over the South Pole. They are caused by the solar wind.**

(15,000,000°C). In the center, the Sun produces its fantastic energy, which keeps it shining brightly. Like all stars, it produces energy by nuclear reactions (see page 28). Hydrogen is the fuel for these reactions.

The stormy surface

We call the glaring surface of the Sun the photosphere (meaning "light-sphere"). It is a boiling, bubbling mass of white-hot gas. It is in constant motion, like a stormy sea. Often great fountains of flaming gas, called prominences, leap high above the surface.

From time to time, dark patches appear on the Sun. These Sunspots are cooler than their surroundings and can grow to be more than 100,000 miles (160,000 km) across. The number of Sunspots visible varies in a regular cycle known as the Sunspot cycle. The maximum number occurs about every 11 years.

Near Sunspots, giant flames called flares often occur, but they usually fade within an hour or two. They give off streams of electrified particles. When these particles reach the Earth, they cause what is sometimes called a magnetic storm. This disrupts long-distance radio communications.

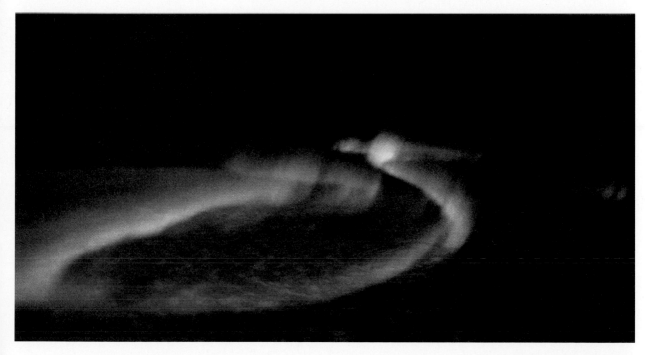

Eclipse of the Sun

The Earth circles around the Sun, and the Moon circles around the Earth, in much the same plane (flat surface). Sometimes the Moon moves in between the Sun and the Earth. Then it blots out some or all of the Sun's light and casts a shadow on the Earth. We call this event an eclipse of the Sun, or a solar eclipse.

Often the Moon covers only part of the Sun. We call this a partial eclipse. The light fades only a little. On rare occasions, the Moon covers the Sun completely. We call this a total eclipse. A total eclipse can be seen over only a small area of the Earth, at most about 150 miles (250 km) across. Outside this area, only a partial eclipse is visible.

During a total eclipse, it takes the Moon about two

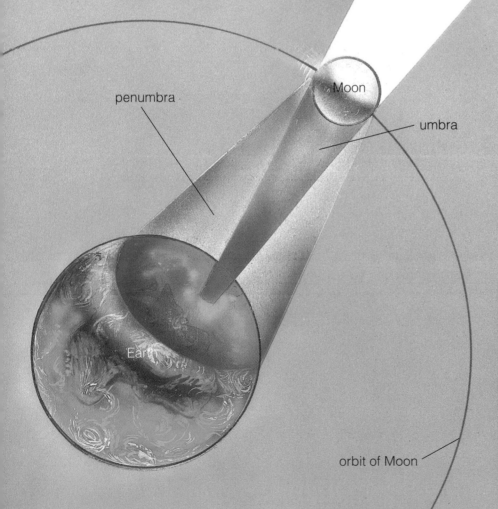

Sunlight

penumbra

Moon

umbra

Earth

orbit of Moon

Eclipses of the Sun take place when the Moon casts a shadow on the Earth. During a total eclipse, a small area of the Earth is in complete darkness (umbra). A much larger area is in partial shadow (penumbra).

What a Coincidence!

The Sun and the Moon appear almost exactly the same size in the sky. The Sun is in fact 400 times bigger than the Moon, but it is 400 times farther away.

hours to pass over the face of the Sun. The Sun is completely covered for only a few minutes, seven at most, during the period known as totality. During totality, the sky darkens, and sometimes gets almost as dark as night. Birds may stop singing and start to roost, and the air sometimes chills.

Observing eclipses

Astronomers travel all over the world to observe total eclipses. It is only during a total eclipse that they can see the Sun's atmosphere.

They watch the Moon gradually cover up the Sun, and look through special filters that protect their eyes. Just before total eclipse, little beads of light appear around the edge of the Moon. These beads, called Baily's Beads, are beams of Sunlight peeping through valleys in the mountains on the Moon.

When the Sun is completely covered, the pink inner atmosphere (chromosphere) becomes visible. Prominences may also be seen. Soon the white outer atmosphere (corona) lights up. Then the beads appear again, indicating that total eclipse is about to end.

1.

2.

Above: **One of the longest total eclipses in recent years took place in Hawaii on July 11, 1991. The Sun remained hidden for over four minutes. These photographs show different stages of that spectacular event.**

1. **The Moon has already taken a big bite out of the Sun.**

2. **The vivid corona lights up during totality.**

Below: **A view of the 1991 total eclipse in Hawaii from the beach at Kona.**

The Moon

On many nights of the year, the Moon helps lighten the darkness. Sometimes it shines bright enough to cast shadows. It shines brighter than the stars and the planets because it is much closer. In fact, it is our nearest neighbor in space, averaging only about 239,000 miles (385,000 km) away. This is a hundred times nearer than the nearest planet, Venus.

The Moon is the Earth's only satellite, which circles around our planet once a month. We know more about the Moon than about any other heavenly body because human beings have traveled to the Moon and explored its surface on foot (see pages 60-61).

The Moon is a very small body. The Earth is nearly four times as big across and has more than eighty times the mass. Being small, the Moon has weak gravity – only one-sixth of the Earth's. Like our own planet, the Moon is made up of rock, but it has no atmosphere, or covering of air, and has no oceans of water. Without air and water, there is no life on the Moon.

Temperatures on the Moon vary greatly. This happens because there is no air to even out the temperature, as happens on Earth. During the day on the Moon, the Sun beats down, making temperatures soar to over boiling point (212°F, 100°C). During the night, temperatures drop as low as –240°F (–150°C).

Below: **The Moon measures about 2,160 miles (3,476 km) across. Here it is compared in size with the United States.**

○ **How big is the Moon?**
○ **What are the phases of the Moon?**
○ **Does the Moon give out its own light?**
○ **Why can we see only one side of the Moon?**
○ **What causes the tides?**

Above: **Even through a small telescope, thousands of craters can be seen on the Moon. The one in the middle of the picture is Copernicus, with Eratosthenes to the right.**

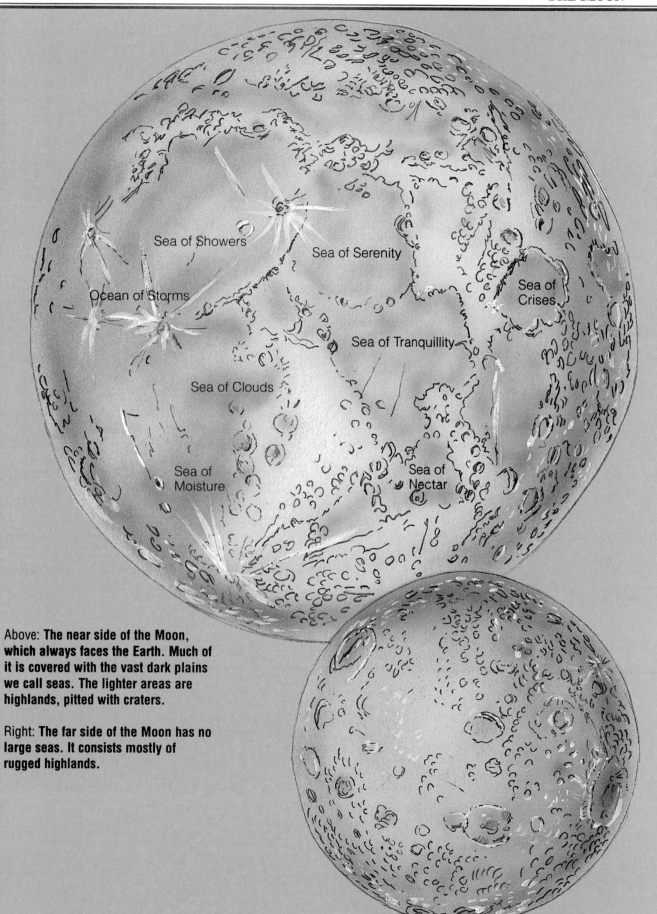

Sea of Showers

Sea of Serenity

Sea of Crises

Ocean of Storms

Sea of Tranquillity

Sea of Clouds

Sea of Moisture

Sea of Nectar

Above: **The near side of the Moon, which always faces the Earth. Much of it is covered with the vast dark plains we call seas. The lighter areas are highlands, pitted with craters.**

Right: **The far side of the Moon has no large seas. It consists mostly of rugged highlands.**

Moonshine

The Moon shines in the night sky, but not by its own light. It shines only because it reflects light from the Sun. If it produced light itself, it would always appear as a full circle in the sky. But, as you know, the Moon appears different as shapes at different times – for example, crescent, half circle, or full circle.

Phases of the Moon

We call the different shapes of the Moon the phases of the Moon. The phases occur because the Sun lights up different parts of the surface as the Moon circles around the Earth each month. The phase we see depends on where the Moon is in relation to the Sun and the Earth.

Lunatics!

It was once believed that mentally ill people were affected by the phases of the Moon. That is why they were called lunatics. *Luna* is the Latin word for "Moon."

Below: **Every month we see the Moon go through its phases as it circles around the Earth. The diagram shows the positions of the Moon in relation to the Sun and the Earth at the four main phases.**

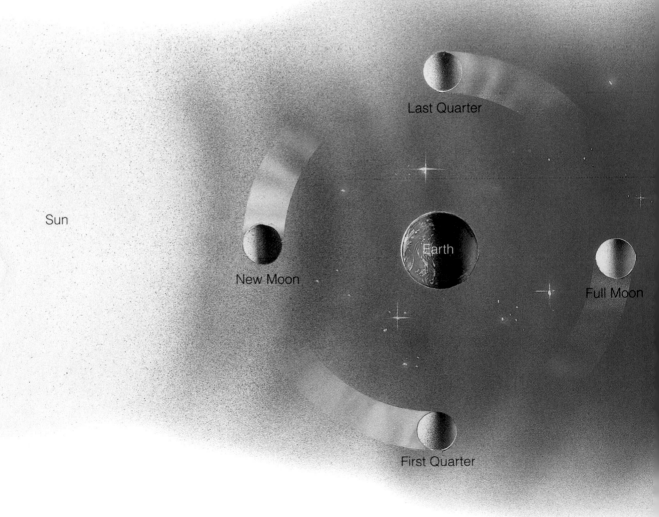

Sun

Last Quarter

New Moon

Earth

Full Moon

First Quarter

Look at the diagram on page 52. When the Moon is directly between the Sun and the Earth, we can't see it at all because no Sunlight falls on the side facing us. This is the new moon phase. After a day or so, the Sun starts to light up the edge of the Moon and we see a slim crescent.

After about a week, half the Moon is lit up (first quarter phase), and after another week the whole face is lit up (full moon). Now the amount of the Moon lit up starts to decrease. After about a week, only half the face is visible (last quarter phase). After another week, only a slim crescent is left, and this disappears at the next new moon.

In all, it takes the Moon 29½ days to go through its phases, from one new Moon to the next. This is one of the natural divisions of time. The months on our calendar are loosely based upon it.

The Moon and the tides

The Moon's gravity is weak, but it still affects the Earth. It causes the tides – the regular rise and fall of the water in the oceans. When the Moon is overhead, it pulls the water toward it. The water level rises and there is a high tide. In other places there is a low tide because the water has been pulled away.

There are two high tides and two low tides about every 24 hours. Look at the diagram (below left). The Moon is overhead at point **A**, so there is a high tide. Also, the Moon pulls the Earth away from the water at point **C**, so point **C** experiences a high tide too. At points **B** and **D**, the water levels have fallen because water has been pulled away into the bulges at **A** and **C**, so **B** and **D** experience a low tide.

About six hours later (below right), the Earth has spun around so that point **B** is facing the Moon. So **B** and **D** now have a high tide, while points **A** and **C** have a low tide.

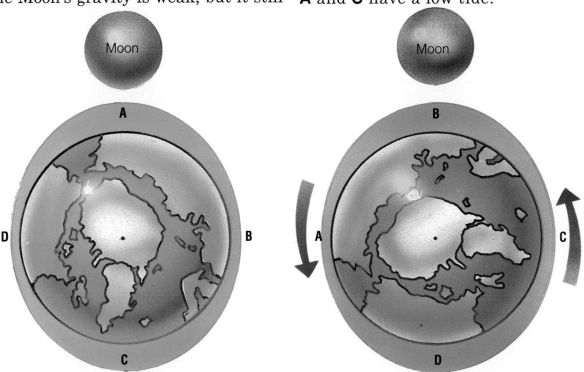

One-faced

When you look at the full moon, you notice that the surface looks exactly the same as it did at the previous full moon and the one before that, and the one before that. In other words, the Moon always presents the same face toward us. We can thus only see half of the Moon's surface, the near side. We can never see the other half, the far side.

How does this come about? It happens because the Moon spins around once as it circles the Earth once.

Like most large heavenly bodies, the Moon has two movements in space. One, it spins on its axis like a top. Two, it travels in orbit around a larger body – in this case the Earth. The Moon spins on its axis once every 27⅓ days. It also travels once around the Earth in 27⅓ days.

The result of these two movements is that the same face of the Moon always points toward us (see the Activity Box on page 55). We call such a movement a captured rotation. Several moons of other planets also have a captured rotation.

A wobbling Moon

Actually, we can see a little more than half the Moon's surface. This is because the Moon appears to

Below: **An eclipse of the Moon takes place when the Sun, the Earth, and the Moon are lined up in space. The Moon goes into partial eclipse when it enters partial shadow (penumbra), and into total eclipse when it enters full shadow (umbra).**

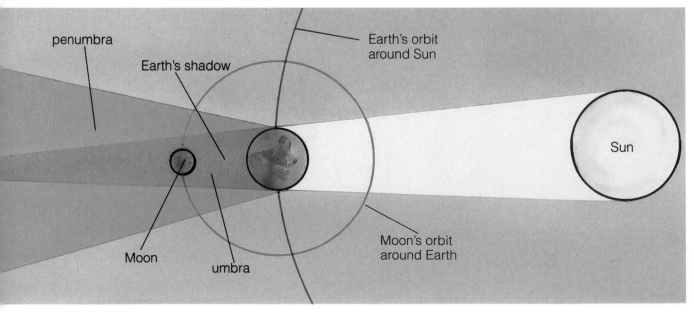

penumbra

Earth's shadow

Earth's orbit around Sun

Sun

Moon

umbra

Moon's orbit around Earth

wobble slightly as it travels around the Earth. Astronomers call these wobbles librations. Because of librations, we can see nearly 60 percent of the Moon's surface at various times.

The Moon in shadow

We see a full moon every month as the Moon goes through its phases. Once or twice a year, the full moon disappears for a few hours. This happens when it moves into the Earth's shadow in space. We call this disappearance an eclipse of the Moon, or a lunar eclipse.

As with a solar eclipse, a lunar eclipse can be partial, with only part of the Moon in shadow. When a lunar eclipse is total, all of the Moon is in shadow. The Moon doesn't completely disappear, however. It is lit up faintly by Sunlight that has been refracted (bent) around the Earth by the atmosphere.

Lunar eclipses last much longer than solar eclipses (see page 48) because the Earth casts a broad shadow. From start to finish, a lunar eclipse can last for up to 3½ hours, and the Moon can stay in total eclipse for 1¾ hours.

During a lunar eclipse, the surface of the Moon takes on a pinkish tint. Many features, such as seas and some craters, can still be seen.

Activity Box

Spinning and circling

Carry out this simple experiment to find out why we always see the same side of the Moon.

Place a ball on a table and think of it as the Earth. Face the ball and think of your face as the Moon. Now walk sideways to your right in a circle around it, always looking at the ball. Stop after you have made a full circle. Do you see what has happened?

Your head has turned around once while you have circled the ball once. Notice that your face always pointed toward the ball.

In space, the Moon turns around once on its axis while it circles once around the Earth. As a result, the same face always points toward the Earth.

The Moon's Surface

○ **What kind of features are seas?**
○ **What are the commonest kinds of Moon rocks?**
○ **Where did the Moon come from?**
○ **What was the Apollo project?**
○ **Who first set foot on the Moon?**
○ **How many Apollo landings were there?**

We can make out some details on the Moon with just our eyes. We can see dark and light areas. When we look at them through a telescope, we can see that the dark areas are vast plains and the light areas are rugged highlands. Early astronomers thought that the dark areas might be seas and the light areas land, and named them *maria* (singular *mare*) and *terrae*, after the Latin words for "seas" and "land."

We still use the terms *sea* or *mare* even though we know these are dry, dusty plains. They all have fanciful names, such as the Sea of Tranquillity (*Mare Tranquillitatis* in Latin) and the Sea of Clouds (*Mare Nubium*). The biggest sea is the Ocean of Storms (*Oceanus Procellarum*). All these seas are on the near side of the Moon, which faces us. There are no large seas on the far side, which we can't see.

The seas were formed when huge lumps of rock hit the Moon long ago. The impacts dug out huge craters, which then filled with molten lava. They are younger than the highlands,which are thought to be part of the Moon's original crust.

Left: **The lunar landscape is barren but very beautiful. Craters large and small are found everywhere. The large one at the top is Ptolemaeus. It is nearly in the center of the Moon as we see it from Earth.**

The highlands include long mountain ranges that soar in places to heights of more than 20,000 feet (6,000 meters). Many of the highest peaks are found in the ranges surrounding the Sea of Showers (*Mare Imbrium*), such as the Apennines, the Caucasus Mountains, and the Alps.

Birth of the Moon

Astronomers used to think that the Moon was once part of the Earth. They believed that it separated from the Earth while our planet was still hot and molten. Most astronomers now think that the Moon and the Earth were formed separately at much the same time, about 4,600 million years ago.

Below: **A wide valley cuts through the lunar mountain range known as the Alps. On either side, there are peaks soaring to 12,000 feet (3,600 meters).**

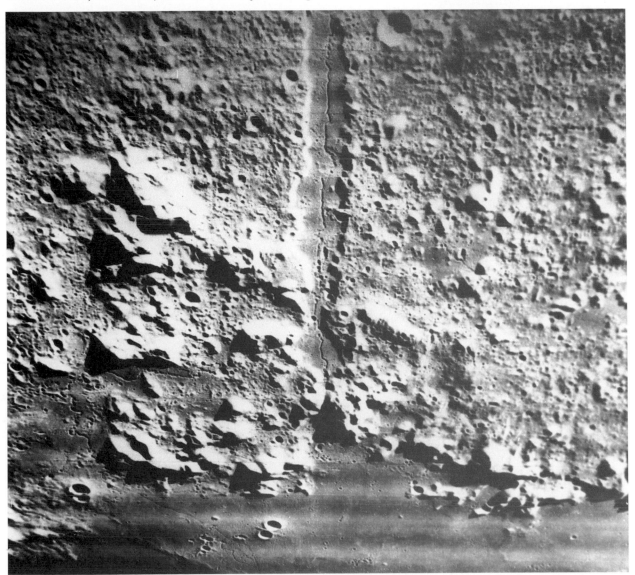

The Lunar Craters

Wherever you look on the Moon's surface, you see craters. These were formed when lumps of rock crashed down onto the Moon from space. They vary in size from small pits to huge holes in the ground that are miles deep and hundreds of miles across. Clavius is one of the biggest, with a diameter of about 145 miles (233 km). The seas have fewer craters than the highlands because they are much younger.

When a large crater formed, the impact caused huge amounts of rocky material to be thrown out in all directions. When Sunlight is reflected from this material, it forms white rays around the crater. At the time of the full Moon, the bright rays around the craters Copernicus and Tycho can easily be seen in binoculars.

Domes, ridges and rills

Many other features appear on the Moon's surface. There are round bulges, or domes, and dimple-like depressions. There are straight and snaking channels called rills that look almost like river beds. Also, there are long raised ridges. All these features are the result of volcanic activity from millions of years ago.

Right: **Astronomers think that the Moon is made up of several layers. Most of the Moon is solid, but a layer near the center may be quite soft.**

Above: **This fine crater on the far side of the Moon measures about 50 miles (80 km) across. Like many large craters, it has mountains in the center.**

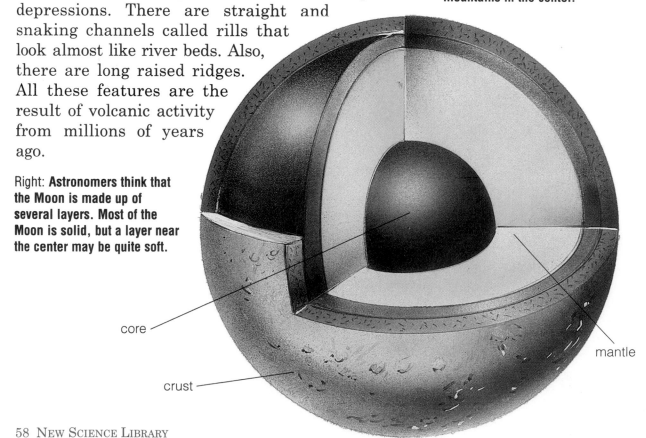

core

crust

mantle

Faults also appear here and there on the surface. They mark where great blocks of the surface have slipped. One of the biggest faults, called the Straight Wall, is found in the Sea of Clouds.

Soil and rocks

Wherever the Apollo astronauts walked on the Moon (see page 61), they found that the surface is covered with dusty soil. They said it is a lot like newly plowed soil on Earth. It is made up of small pieces of rock and usually contains tiny balls of glass. This makes the surface slippery to walk on.

The rocks the astronauts brought back proved to be of two main kinds. There were volcanic rocks, much like the basalt rocks we find on Earth. Many were dark in color and riddled with holes where gases had escaped. The other kind of rock was made up of large and small rock chips cemented together with lava. This kind of rock, called breccia, is also common on Earth.

Moon rocks are made up of much the same minerals as Earth rocks, but the minerals are present in different proportions. Many Moon rocks are richer in certain metals, including titanium, chromium, and uranium.

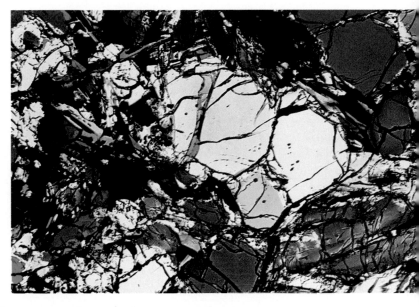

Above: **Crystals show up as different colors in a thin slice of Moon rock. The picture was taken using a special rock microscope.**

Below: **This is a common kind of Moon rock called breccia. It is made up of chips of old rocks cemented together.**

Above: **This kind of Moon rock is called basalt. It was formed when volcanoes erupted on the Moon millions of years ago.**

Destination Moon

"One small step ..."

As Neil Armstrong stepped down on to the Moon, he said: "That's one small step for a man, one giant leap for mankind."

On July 20, 1969, a human being from planet Earth first set foot on another world, the Moon. He was Neil Armstrong. The first of 12 U.S. Apollo astronauts who walked on the Moon, in the greatest feat of exploration there has ever been.

In a speech to Congress in May 1961, President John F. Kennedy urged Americans to land a man on the Moon. This signaled the birth of NASA's Apollo Moon landing project. To achieve this aim, NASA had to design, build, and test all kinds of new equipment. The biggest piece of hardware was the Saturn, a gigantic rocket powerful enough to boost the Apollo spacecraft toward the Moon (see page 91).

In all, there were six Apollo landings.

Apollo Moon Landings

Apollo 11
July 16-24, 1969
N. Armstrong, E. Aldrin, M. Collins
Sea of Tranquillity

Apollo 12
November 14-24, 1969
C. Conrad, A.L. Bean, R.F. Gordon
Ocean of Storms

Apollo 14
January 31 - February 9, 1971
A.B. Shepard, E.D. Mitchell, S.D. Roosa
Fra Mauro formation

Apollo 15
July 26 - August 7, 1971
D.R. Scott, J.B. Irwin, A.M. Worden
Foothills of Apennines

Apollo 16
April 16-27, 1972
J.W. Young, C.M. Duke, T.K. Mattingly
Descartes highlands

Apollo 17
December 7-19, 1972
E.A. Cernan, H.H. Schmitt, R. Evans
Taurus-Littrow valley

Below: **The Apollo 8 astronauts were the first to orbit the Moon and see the Earth rise over the lunar horizon. They blazed the trail to the Moon in December 1968.**

They set down the astronauts in varied landscapes – on the dusty seas and in the rugged highlands. The astronauts spent a total of 80 hours exploring the lunar surface. The last three teams were able to explore wider areas because they had transportation in the form of a battery – powered "Moon buggy."

The astronauts carried out many experiments on the Moon and set up several automatic scientific stations. The instruments they used included seismometers, which were designed to record Moonquakes, or slight shaking of the ground. Other instruments included laser reflectors. By reflecting beams of laser light from them, scientists on Earth can calculate exactly how far away the Moon is at any time.

Eugene Cernan was last to leave the Moon in December 1972, promising: "God willing, we shall return with peace and hope for all mankind."

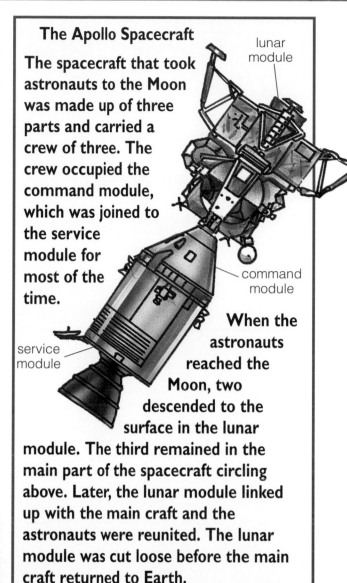

The Apollo Spacecraft

The spacecraft that took astronauts to the Moon was made up of three parts and carried a crew of three. The crew occupied the command module, which was joined to the service module for most of the time.

When the astronauts reached the Moon, two descended to the surface in the lunar module. The third remained in the main part of the spacecraft circling above. Later, the lunar module linked up with the main craft and the astronauts were reunited. The lunar module was cut loose before the main craft returned to Earth.

Above: **Apollo 17 astronaut Harrison Schmitt, who is a geologist, collects samples near a huge boulder in the Taurus-Littrow valley.**

Right: **The Apollo 15 astronauts were the first to use the four-wheeled moon buggy.**

○ **What is a falling star?**
○ **What is a meteorite?**
○ **Where is Meteor Crater?**
○ **What are comets made of?**
○ **Where is the asteroid belt?**
○ **Which is the biggest asteroid?**

Bits and Pieces

If you gaze at the night sky for long enough, you are almost certain to see a shooting star. This is a streak of light that looks like a star falling out of the sky. It isn't, of course. In fact it is a meteor, a speck of rock from outer space burning up as it passes through the Earth's atmosphere.

The space between the planets in our Solar System is full of specks and lumps of rock. We call these particles meteoroids. Most are little bigger than grains of sand. When they get near the Earth, they are attracted by gravity and enter the atmosphere as meteors.

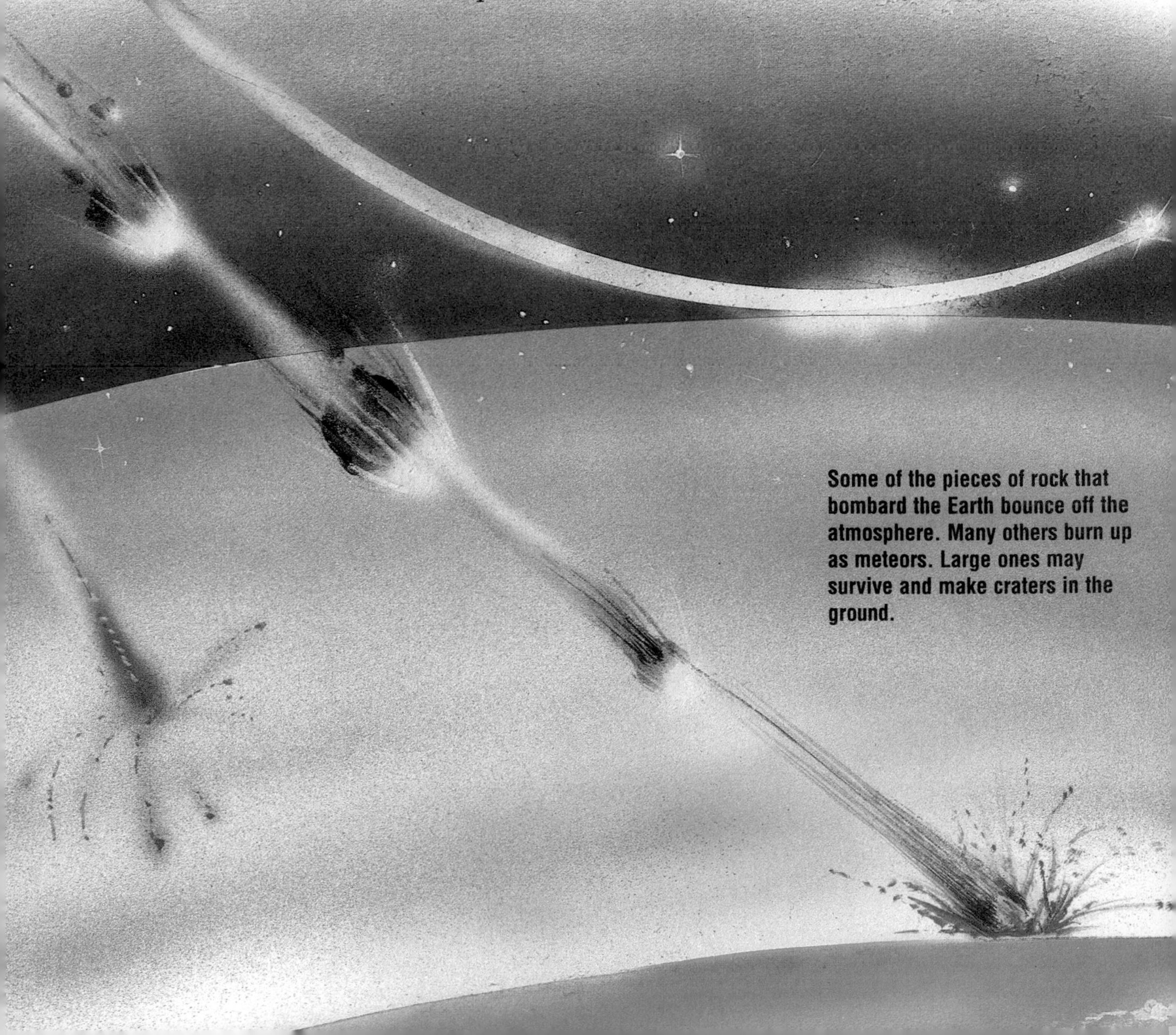

Some of the pieces of rock that bombard the Earth bounce off the atmosphere. Many others burn up as meteors. Large ones may survive and make craters in the ground.

Right: **Meteor Crater in the Arizona Desert is the most famous crater on Earth. It is 1,383 yards (1,265 meters) in diameter and 191 yards (175 meters) deep.**

Meteors travel very fast – at speeds up to 160,000 mph (260 km/h). At such speeds they get very hot because of friction with the air. Small meteor particles melt and burn up, creating streaks of light. They turn into fine dust, which gradually falls to Earth.

When larger meteor particles melt and start to burn, they create trails that can often be seen in daylight. We call them fireballs. Some lumps survive and fall to the ground, as meteorites. If they are large enough, they can make big craters. Many meteorites are made up mostly of rock, but some are mostly metal, made up of a mixture of iron and nickel.

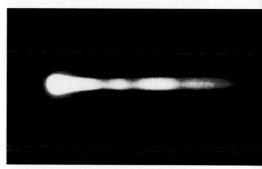

Above: **This fiery trail was left by a large meteorite falling to Earth. Its outer surface was melting because of the fierce heat.**

Meteors galore

On most nights you might see about five or six meteors every hour. At certain times of the year, you could see as many as 60 an hour. This happens when a meteor shower occurs. During a shower, all the meteors appear to come from a certain point in the sky, called the radiant.

Each shower is named after the star constellation in which the radiant is located. One of the best showers is the Perseid, named because it is located in the constellation Perseus. It takes place regularly in August each year.

Tons Down

Every minute, day and night, about 10 tons (9 tonnes) of dust from burned-up meteors fall down to the Earth.

Comets

The fiery streaks of meteors light up the night sky for just a few seconds. Other visitors to our skies stay around much longer and can be bright enough to blot out the stars. They are comets. Comets often appear in the sky without warning, and ancient peoples would become frightened when this happened. They therefore regarded comets as bringers of bad luck, disasters, wars, and famine.

Most asteroids circle in space between the orbits of the planets Mars and Jupiter. A few travel farther afield.

Comets journey in toward the Sun from great distances. Some appear regularly, others maybe only once. Note that the comet's tail always points away from the Sun.

For most of the time, the bodies we call comets remain invisible, traveling far away in the depths of the Solar System. They become visible only when they wander in toward the Sun. They are lumps of rock, dust, and ice and are often described as "dirty snowballs."

As they get closer to the Sun, the Sun's heat makes some of their ice melt and turn to gas. This releases some of their dust. A cloud of gas and dust gathers around the comet. This reflects Sunlight and makes the comet visible.

As the comet travels closer to the Sun, more gas and dust are given off. The comet gets brighter and also grows a "tail." The tail is formed by glowing gas and dust. This has been pushed away from the head of the comet by the pressure of the solar wind (see page 46), the stream of particles given off by the Sun.

Regular visitors

Some comets appear in our skies at regular intervals. We call them periodic comets. Encke's comet puts in an appearance every three years or so. Halley's comet appears about every 76 years. It last appeared in 1986 and is expected to be seen again around the year 2061.

The asteroids

Even larger rocky lumps than comets are found in the space between the orbits of Mars and Jupiter. They are the asteroids, also called the minor planets. Fortunately for us, most of them stay there, occupying a broad band we call the asteroid belt.

The largest asteroid, Ceres, is about 600 miles (1,000 km) across. It and the other asteroids are too small to be seen from Earth with the naked eye.

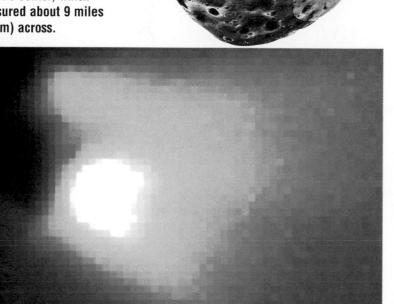

Asteroids are of all shapes and sizes. This tiny Martian Moon, Phobos, was probably once an asteroid.

Below: **Five space probes were sent to meet Halley's comet in 1986. The European probe Giotto passed a few hundred miles away and took spectacular close-up pictures of the comet's center, which measured about 9 miles (15 km) across.**

King Harold's Comet

Halley's comet appeared in Earth's skies in 1066, at the time the French invaded England. This event was recorded in the famous Bayeux tapestry (above). At the time, people believed that comets brought bad luck. So it proved for the English king Harold, who was killed by an arrow in the eye.

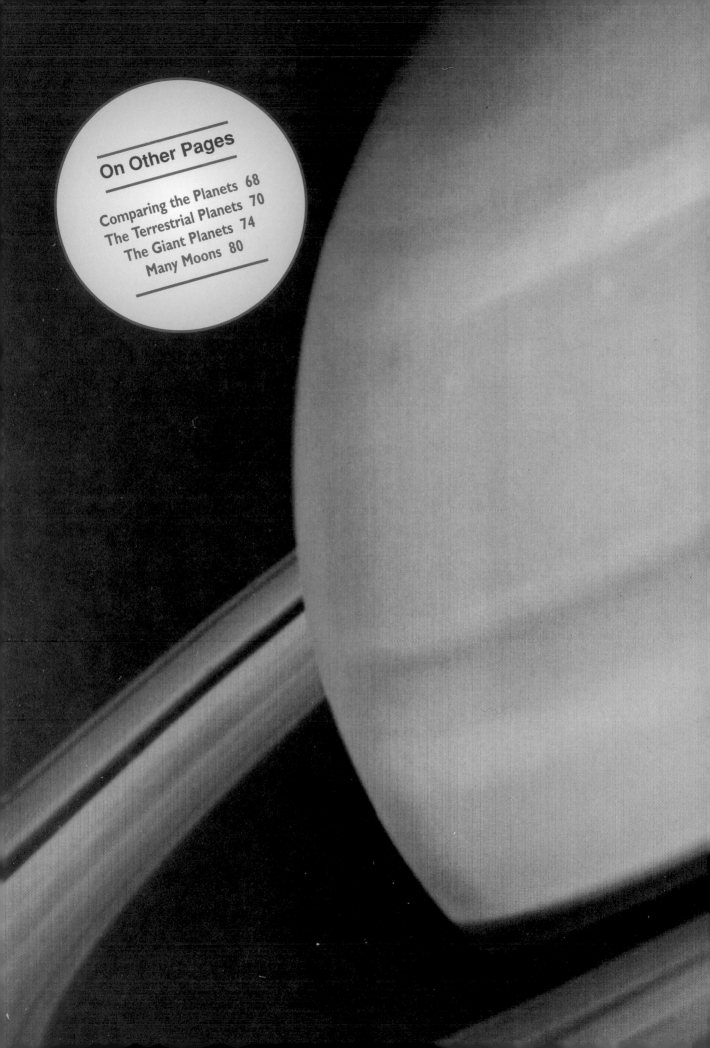

4 The Planets

From Earth, the planet we live on, we can see five of the other eight planets with the naked eye. In order of distance from the Sun, they are Mercury, Venus, Mars, Jupiter, and Saturn.

These planets look like stars, but often shine much brighter than the brightest stars. While the real stars remain fixed in the same positions in the constellations, the planets wander about. The word *planet*, in fact, means "wanderer."

Three more planets are too far away for us to see with the naked eye – Uranus, Neptune, and Pluto. They were discovered within the last 250 years, Pluto as recently as 1930.

All the nine planets are very different from each other, but they are divided into two distinct groups. The four planets closest to the Sun (Mercury to Mars) are relatively small rocky bodies. We call them the terrestrial, or Earth-like, planets.

The next four planets out (Jupiter to Neptune) could hardly be more different. They are gigantic in size and made up mainly of gas. They are also surrounded by systems of rings and have many satellites (Moons) circling around them. The odd planet out is the outermost one, Pluto, which doesn't belong to either group.

Over the past 30 years, our knowledge of the planets has expanded enormously. This is because space probes have visited them all (see pages 110–121), except Pluto. They have sent back spectacular close-up pictures of worlds we can't yet visit ourselves.

Saturn and its rings, one of the most glorious sights in the Solar System. This beautiful image is one of the many thousands that the Voyager probes sent back when they explored the giant planets.

Comparing the Planets

On these pages we present some essential information about the nine planets. The diagram below illustrates the enormous difference in size between the terrestrial planets and the giants. The king of the planets, Jupiter, could swallow over 1,300 Earths. Yet note how small it is compared with the size of the Sun.

For a numerical comparison of the planets, look at the data in the table opposite. First read the following notes.

Diameter: The diameter of each planet is measured at the equator. The planets tend to bulge slightly at the equator because of their rotation.

Spin: Each planet rotates, or spins, on its axis. The Earth spins on its axis once about every 24 hours, the period we call a day. Each planet spins around at a different speed. Some have a shorter day than Earth, others a longer one.

Distance: The planets circle at widely different distances from the Sun. These figures give average distances. The actual distance of a planet from the Sun varies.

Circling the Sun: Because the planets lie at different distances from the Sun, they take different lengths of time to circle around it. The Earth circles around the Sun in a little over 365 days, the period we call a year. The year on other planets varies widely.

Orbits: The planets do not literally travel in circles around the Sun. They travel in elliptical orbits, or paths in the shape of an ellipse (see diagram above). This explains why their distance from the Sun varies from time to time.

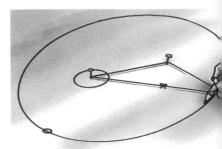

Planets travel around the Sun in a path that has the shape of an ellipse. To draw an ellipse, place two pins on a piece of cardboard and loop a piece of string around them as shown. Put a pencil through the loop and draw a line on the cardboard. The line will follow the shape of an ellipse.

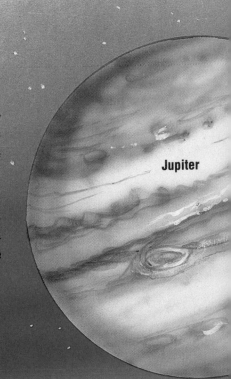

Jupiter

Mercury

Venus

Earth

Mars

Sun

Planet	Mercury	Venus	Earth	Mars	Jupiter	Saturn	Uranus	Neptune	Pluto
Diameter at equator (mi) (km)	3,031 4,878	7,521 12,104	7,926 12,756	4,222 6,794	88,400 142,200	74,600 120,000	31,800 51,200	30,800 49,500	1,420 2,284
Spins on axis in (days/hours)	58.7 d	243 d	23.9 h	24.6 h	9.8 h	10.2 h	16.3 h	16.0 h	6.3 d
Av. distance from Sun (million mi) (million km)	36 57.9	67.2 108.2	93 149.6	141.6 227.9	483.6 778.3	887 1,427	1,783 2,870	2,794 4,497	3,666 5,900
Circles Sun in (days/years)	88 d	224.7 d	365.2 d	687 d	11.9 y	29.5 y	84 y	164.8 y	247.7 y
Mass (Earth=1)	0.06	0.82	1	0.11	318	95	14.6	17.2	0.002
Density (Water=1)	5.4	5.2	5.5	3.9	1.3	0.7	1.3	1.8	2
Volume (Earth=1)	0.05	0.88	1	0.15	1,319	744	67	57	0.0005
Surface gravity (Earth=1)	0.38	0.90	1	0.38	2.64	1.2	1.2	1.2	0.15
No. of Moons	0	0	1	2	16+	22+	15+	8	1

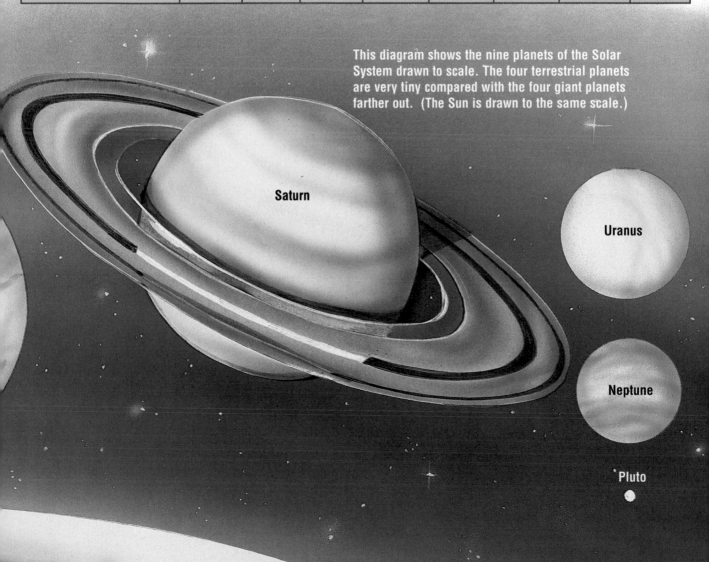

This diagram shows the nine planets of the Solar System drawn to scale. The four terrestrial planets are very tiny compared with the four giant planets farther out. (The Sun is drawn to the same scale.)

Saturn

Uranus

Neptune

Pluto

The Terrestrial Planets

- ○ What does Mercury look like?
- ○ Does Mercury have an atmosphere?
- ○ Why can't we see the surface of Venus?
- ○ What is the main gas in Venus's atmosphere?
- ○ Are there continents on Venus?
- ○ Why is Mars called the Red Planet?
- ○ How big is Mars's Grand Canyon?
- ○ Is there or has there been life on Mars?

Mercury is the second smallest of the planets, not much bigger than the Moon. It is not an easy planet to find in the sky because it stays close to the Sun. You can sometimes see it in the east just before Sunrise, or in the west just after Sunset. It looks like a pinkish star. Even through a telescope, you can make out few details of the planet's surface.

Close-up pictures of Mercury from space show that the planet is covered with craters and looks much like the Moon. The major difference between the two bodies is that Mercury has no large flat plains, or seas, like the Moon. Mercury resembles the Moon in another way. Because it is so small, its gravity is weak, so it has not been able to hold on to an atmosphere like other planets.

Mercury spins on its axis very slowly. This means that the side facing the Sun stays lit up for months at a time. This causes its temperature to soar to over 850°F (450°C). The other side of Mercury remains dark for months at a time, and there the temperature can drop as low as −290°F (−180°C).

Evening star, morning star

Of all the planets, Venus is the easiest to recognize. On many evenings at Sunset we see it shining brightly in the western sky as the evening star. At other times we see it shining in the eastern sky at dawn as the morning star.

Venus shines brighter than any other planet for two reasons. First, it is the planet that comes closest to Earth, sometimes within 26

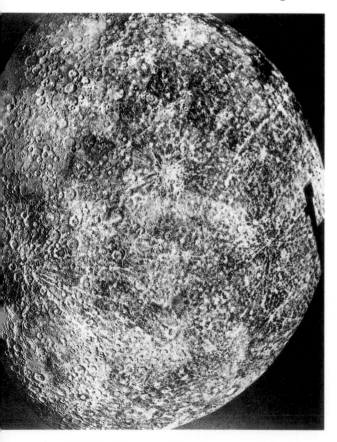

Left: **The Sun-baked surface of Mercury is covered in craters. This picture was taken by the Mariner 10 space probe in 1974 from a distance of about 49,000 miles (79,000 km).**

Right: **If you look at Venus through a telescope, you can see its different phases. The planet appears to be a different size at each phase as it travels toward or away from the Earth.**

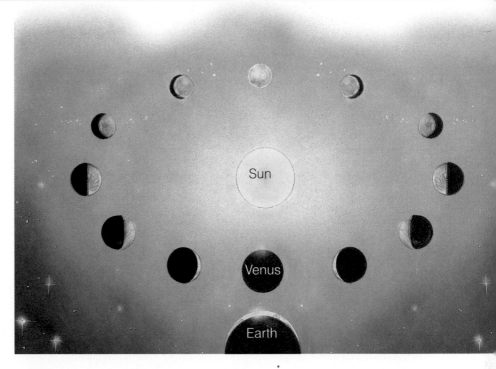

What a Way to Go!

Venus is not a very pleasant place for humans. If they were accidentally transported there, they would be killed instantly because they would at the same time be suffocated, crushed, and roasted.

million miles (42 million km). Second, it is permanently covered with thick clouds, which reflect Sunlight brilliantly.

In size, Venus is a near twin of the Earth, being only slightly smaller. It also has an atmosphere. It is relatively close to us in the Solar System. We might think, therefore, that Venus would be a similar planet to the Earth, but nothing could be farther from the truth.

Venus's greenhouse

The atmosphere on Venus does not contain oxygen and is made up mostly of carbon dioxide gas. Its pressure is more than 90 times atmospheric pressure on Earth. The carbon dioxide gas has the effect of trapping the Sun's heat like a greenhouse. As a result, the temperature on Venus is a scorching 900°F (480°C), which is hot enough to melt lead.

Until recently, we have not been able to see Venus's surface because of the thick clouds in the atmosphere. Radar scans by space probes have now shown the planet to have a varied and fascinating surface. Much of the planet is low-lying, but there are two large higher regions, or continents. One, called Aphrodite Terra, is about the size of Africa. The other is called Ishtar Terra, and is about the size of Australia.

Canals on Mars

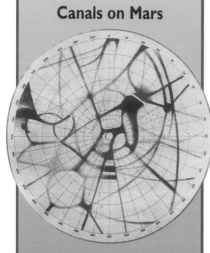

In the 19th century, many people believed, or wanted to believe, that there was life on Mars. The idea gained ground after 1877, when the Italian astronomer Giovanni Schiaparelli announced he had seen "canali," meaning "channels," on Mars. This was mistranslated as "canals," meaning "artificial waterways." People then began to imagine a dying Martian race, building canals to carry water from the melting polar ice caps to the equator, where it was warm enough to farm crops. Space probes have found no signs of canals or any other evidence of life on Mars.

The Red Planet

Mars is another planet that is easy to spot in the night sky. It is called the Red Planet because of its fiery red-orange color.

Mars comes closer to Earth than any other planet except Venus. At times it comes within 35 million miles (56 million km). It is similar to Earth in some respects. A day on Mars is only slightly longer than our own day. The planet has an atmosphere, and it also has seasons like the Earth, only they are almost twice as long as ours. It has ice caps at the north and south poles, like Earth. They shrink in summer and grow again in winter.

However, Mars is different from the Earth in most other ways. It lies much farther from the Sun and is much colder. Temperatures do not often rise above freezing, even in summer. It has only a very thin atmosphere, made up mainly of carbon dioxide gas.

Some people used to think that there might be some form of life on Mars, but conditions there are not suitable for life as we know it to survive.

The spectacular landscape

The landscape on Mars is varied and, in some parts,

Olympus Mons is the biggest volcano we know in the Solar System.

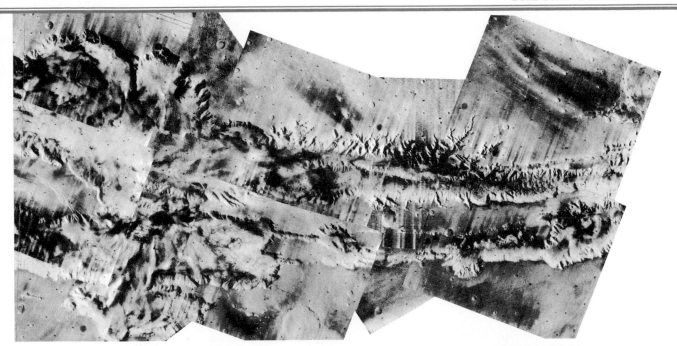

truly spectacular. There are large cratered regions, sandy deserts, broad basins, and mountain ranges. An upland region called the Tharsis Ridge boasts three huge extinct volcanoes up to 12 miles (20 km) high. Nearby is an even higher volcano, Olympus Mons.

Water and weather

There is no running water on Mars, but there is water vapor in the air. It forms into mist and clouds in mountainous and canyon regions. The water vapor also freezes into ice at the poles, forming the ice caps.

A notable feature of the weather on Mars is dust storms. They occur frequently in the atmosphere, which is a hundred times thinner than that on Earth.

Above: **This is Mars's Grand Canyon, which is named Valles Marineris. It runs for 3,000 miles (5,000 km) near the planet's equator.**

Below: **The surface of Mars is orange in color. In places it is covered with a kind of sandy soil and small rocks.**

Jupiter is perhaps the most colorful of the planets. Bands of colored clouds race around its thick atmosphere. In this picture, Jupiter's large moons– Io and Europa are passing over the planet's face. They are two of at least 16 moons circling Jupiter.

The Giant Planets

○ Why is Jupiter so bright?
○ What is the **Great Red Spot?**
○ Why do **Saturn's rings** sometimes disappear?
○ Why didn't ancient **astronomers know about Uranus?**
○ Why is **Uranus** sometimes called the topsy-turvy planet?
○ Why is **Neptune** sometimes the farthest planet?
○ Which planet was discovered in the 20th century?

Jupiter is the nearest of four giant planets in the outer Solar System. It often appears as bright as Mars in the night sky, but you can easily tell them apart because Jupiter is brilliant white, while Mars is distinctly red. Jupiter appears bright even though it lies more than five times farther away than Mars. That is because it very large and is covered with clouds that reflect light well.

Jupiter is truly gigantic, with 11 times the diameter and more than 300 times the mass of the Earth. It is by far the biggest planet in the whole Solar System.

Zones, belts, and spots

Through a telescope, you can see light and dark bands covering the disk (face) of Jupiter. Astronomers call the light bands zones and the dark ones belts. They are clouds that have been drawn out into bands by the rapid rotation of the planet. The

Jupiter Under Attack

In March 1993, U.S. comet spotters Carolyn Shoemaker and David Levy photographed a new comet, which became known as Shoemaker Levy 9. It was, in fact, a string of fragments from a larger body that had broken up the previous year.

What was exciting about this comet was that it was headed for a collision with Jupiter. Calculations showed that the comet fragments would start crashing into Jupiter on July 16, 1994.

The bombardment began right on schedule. Over the next few days, 24 comet fragments the size of mountains pounded Jupiter. They released fantastic energy, equivalent to hundreds of hydrogen bombs exploding together. New spots appeared on the planet, showing where the collisions took place.

This picture shows the clouds swirling about near the Great Red Spot. This is a very stormy part of Jupiter's atmosphere.

planet rotates faster than any other planet, rotating once in less than 10 hours.

Many other details are visible on Jupiter's disk, including spots and wavy swirls. The biggest spot is deep red in color and is a permanent feature. Called the Great Red Spot, it is a gigantic hurricane-like storm measuring more than 17,000 miles (28,000 km) across.

In fact, violent storms occur frequently throughout Jupiter's thick atmosphere, and, like violent storms on Earth, they are accompanied by lightning. The Voyager space probes recorded vivid bolts of lightning when they viewed the night side of Jupiter.

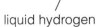

atmosphere

liquid metallic hydrogen

rocky core

liquid hydrogen

Jupiter's atmosphere is made up mainly of hydrogen gas. The clouds are formed of water and ammonia droplets and ice crystals. Beneath the atmosphere are layers of liquid hydrogen and liquid metallic hydrogen. Hydrogen becomes a kind of metal when it is under very great pressure. The rocky core at the center of Jupiter is about the size of the Earth.

Rings around Jupiter

The Voyager probes also found that Jupiter has a very strong magnetic field. This field extends far out into space and traps electrified particles in large donut-shaped regions. These regions are the source of intense radiation that could pose a real danger to space travelers in the future. Jupiter also has a ring that is similar to the kinds of rings Saturn has, which are made up of small lumps of rock and ice whizzing around the planet at high speed.

Saturn's rings

Through a telescope, we can't see Jupiter's ring, but Saturn's rings look magnificent. They form a flat disk around the planet's equator. From one side to the other, they measure 168,000 miles (270,000 km) across, or more than twice Saturn's diameter.

We can make out three distinct rings, named A, B, and C. The outer A ring is separated from the B ring by a gap known as the Cassini division. The Voyager probes discovered several more rings and found that the three main rings are made up of hundreds of separate ringlets.

Saturn's disk

Saturn is the most distant planet we can see with the naked eye, but we need a telescope to see its rings. Large telescopes reveal that its disk is crossed with parallel bands, but they are much fainter than those on Jupiter. The bands are fast-moving clouds, driven by winds that blow at speeds of more than 1,100 mph (1,800 km/h). Many spots and swirls can be seen on the

---

Lighter Than Water

Saturn's relative density is only 0.7, so if you could put it in an enormous bowl of water, it would float!

Saturn and its beautiful ring system. Note that the middle B ring is the brightest. Some of its ringlets can be seen. So can mysterious dark spoke-like features.

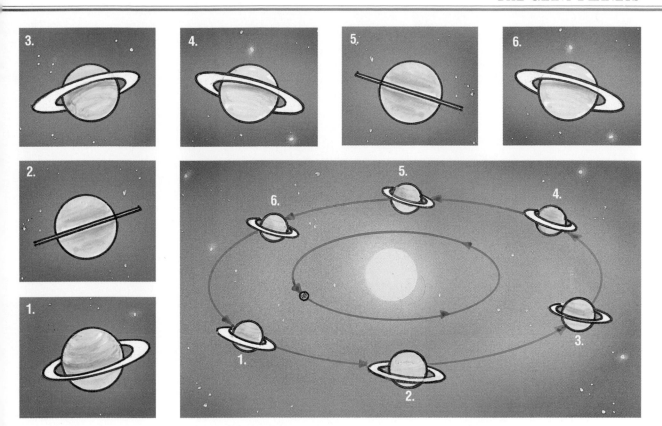

disk, where violent storms take place. However, they are not as big nor as long-lasting as Jupiter's Great Red Spot.

Saturn, then, is a smaller and paler version of Jupiter, and is thought to be much like Jupiter in makeup (see page 75). It too has a strong magnetic field and radiation belts.

Like all planets, Saturn spins on its axis. This axis is tilted in relation to the orbit it takes around the Sun. This means that from Earth we see the rings at different angles at different times. When we see them edge-on, they almost disappear from view.

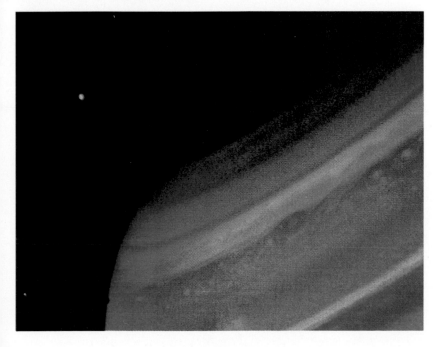

Two of Saturn's many Moons (at least 22) show up in this false-color picture. They are Tethys (top) and Enceladus. False-color processing has been used here to bring out features in Saturn's atmosphere.

Remote Worlds

Way beyond Saturn in the depths of the Solar System lie another three planets, which are visible only through a telescope. They are Uranus, Neptune, and Pluto.

The English astronomer William Herschel discovered Uranus in 1781, after first thinking it was a comet. The new planet proved to be twice as far away from the Sun as Saturn, at a distance of nearly 2 billion miles (3 billion km).

Bland Uranus

Through a telescope, Uranus looks like a featureless bluish-green disk. Close-up photographs of the planet taken by Voyager 2 show no features either. However, Voyager photographs did show a set of narrow rings around the planet. These rings, at least 10 in all, had earlier been spotted from Earth.

The deep atmosphere of Uranus is made up mostly of hydrogen. Beneath the atmosphere there is thought to be a great hot ocean of water and ammonia. At the center is a core of rock and iron about the size of the Earth.

Above: **Like all planets, Uranus has two motions in space. It spins on its axis as it travels in orbit around the Sun. The peculiar thing about Uranus is that its axis is tilted all the way over in relation to its orbit. Whereas the other planets spin almost upright like a top, Uranus spins on its side.**

Colorful Neptune

Soon after Uranus had been discovered, astronomers

Left: **The bluish-green color of Uranus is due to methane being present in the atmosphere.**

found that its orbit was somewhat irregular. It appeared as if another planet farther out was affecting it. In 1846 the German astronomer Johann Galle spotted the planet, which was named Neptune. It proved to be nearly identical in size to Uranus.

Because Neptune is so far away, little was known about it until Voyager 2 sped by it in 1989. The planet is a deep blue color and shows interesting features, such as dark spots and white wisps. The dark spots appear to be storm centers; the white wisps appear to be clouds.

Voyager 2 also spotted a set of faint rings around Neptune. This means that all four giant planets have ring systems, but only Saturn's rings can be seen from Earth.

The Farthest Planet?

Neptune is at present the most distant planet. This is because Pluto is now traveling inside Neptune's orbit. Not until 1999 will Pluto start traveling outside Neptune's orbit and become the most distant planet again.

Above left: **Storms and clouds dot the disk of Neptune. Astronomers are surprised to find so much activity in the atmosphere of a planet so far from the Sun.**

The ninth planet

An American astronomer, Clyde Tombaugh, discovered the ninth planet as recently as 1930. It was named Pluto. Pluto lies an average of nearly 4 billion miles (6 billion km) from the Sun and takes nearly 250 years to circle once around the Sun. It is a very tiny world, much smaller even than the Moon. It is probably made up of rock and ice, and may have an atmosphere of methane.

Right: **Even in large telescopes, Pluto (arrowed) is only a pinpoint of light. It can be spotted as it travels against the background of stars.**

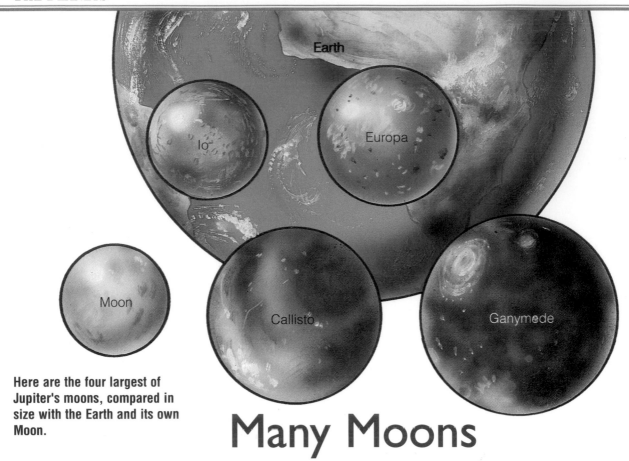

Here are the four largest of Jupiter's moons, compared in size with the Earth and its own Moon.

Many Moons

○ **Which Moon has volcanoes?**
○ **Which Moon has an atmosphere?**
○ **What is odd about Miranda, a moon of Uranus?**

Earth travels through space with a close companion – its satellite, the Moon. All the planets except Mercury and Venus have satellites, or moons, too.

Mars has only two tiny moons, Phobos and Deimos. Even the biggest, Phobos, is only about 20 miles (30 km) across. Tiny Pluto has a moon, named Charon, which surprisingly is half the size of Pluto.

The four giant planets have among them the most moons – at least 61. Many of the moons are tiny and were discovered only when space probes visited the planets. Jupiter alone has at least 16 moons, Saturn no less than 22, Uranus at least 15, and Neptune 8.

The four biggest moons of Jupiter – Io, Europa, Ganymede, and Callisto – can clearly be seen through binoculars. Ganymede has a diameter of 3,278 miles (5,276 km) and is one of the biggest moons in the Solar System. It is bigger than the planet Mercury. So is Saturn's largest moon, Titan (3,194 miles, 5,140 km diameter). Titan is interesting because it is the only moon with an atmosphere.

Above: **Saturn's Moon Dione is peppered with impact craters.**

Background picture: **Ganymede's surface has curious grooves and bright icy craters.**

Above: **Io, Jupiter's most colorful moon, has live volcanoes.**

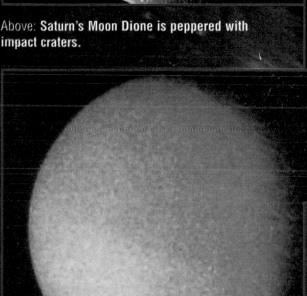

Above: **Titan's atmosphere is made up mainly of nitrogen and methane.**

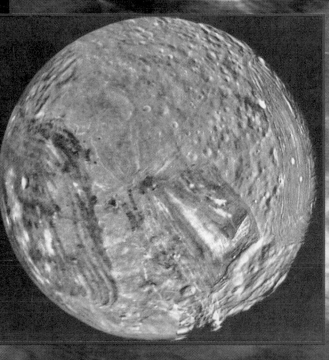

Right: **Miranda has a peculiar surface. It looks as if the moon was once smashed into pieces, which then came together again.**

On Other Pages

5 Space Travel

On October 4, 1957, the Earth gained an extra Moon, or satellite. It was an artificial satellite launched into space by Russian scientists. The launch of this satellite, named Sputnik 1, marked the beginning of the Space Age.

The United States launched its first satellite on January 31, 1958. Named Explorer 1, it made the first scientific discovery of the Space Age. It found huge bands of radiation around the Earth. These bands are now called the Van Allen Belts.

Explorer 1 was launched from Cape Canaveral in Florida, a site that has expanded into the world's most famous spaceport, the Kennedy Space Center. Leading the team that launched Explorer was Wernher von Braun. He pioneered the development of the powerful V-2 rocket in Germany during World War Two. He went on to design the Saturn V rocket that, in the 1960s, took U.S. astronauts to the Moon.

This chapter looks at the problems of getting into space and the methods of doing so. We shall see that rockets hold the key to space flight. The first person to realize this was a deaf Russian school teacher named Konstantin Tsiolkovsky, back in the 1870s. He even suggested using rockets burning hydrogen and oxygen like the shuttle does today. He is now considered the father of astronautics, the science of space travel.

This picture shows the spectacular launch of the Saturn V Moon rocket that would propel Apollo 15 astronauts to the Moon. The Saturn V was the biggest rocket ever, measuring 363 feet (111 meters) overall. It is unlikely that any rocket this size will ever be built again.

Getting into Space

On Earth we live at the bottom of a great ocean of air we call the atmosphere. It is thickest at sea level, but gradually thins as you rise higher.

When you reach a height of about 100 miles (160 km), there is scarcely any air left at all. You are on the edge of the atmosphere and are entering the airless world of space.

The atmosphere is kept in place around the Earth by gravity. Gravity is the force with which the Earth attracts everything on it and near it. The force of gravity keeps your feet on the ground and makes things fall when you let go of them. It is a very strong force – strong enough, for example, to hold the Moon in its path around the Earth.

Beating gravity

To get into space, we must somehow overcome gravity. How can we do this? You can gain a clue by throwing a ball. The faster you throw it, the farther it travels before it falls to the ground. You are beginning to overcome gravity with speed. Speed holds the key to getting into space.

Right: **The Earth's atmosphere is thickest at the bottom, in a layer we call the troposphere. Above that is the stratosphere, the part that contains the ozone layer, which filters out harmful rays from the Sun. In the ionosphere, minute traces of air exist in the form of electrically charged particles called ions. The ionosphere gradually merges into space.**

250

200

150

100

ionosphere

50

30

stratosphere

mesosphere

0
miles

troposphere

○ **Where does space begin?**
○ **How can we beat gravity?**
○ **What is orbital velocity?**
○ **What is interesting about a geostationary orbit?**
○ **What is escape velocity?**

Imagine you are standing on a high mountain and that you can throw a ball as fast as you like. The faster you throw it, the farther it goes before it falls back to Earth. If you could throw the ball at a speed of 17,500 mph (28,000 km/h), a strange thing would happen. The ball would fall in a curving path that matched the curve of the Earth, remaining at the same height above the ground. In other words, it would become a satellite of the Earth, traveling round and round in a constant path, or orbit.

Orbital velocity

To put any object into orbit as a satellite, we have to launch it at a speed of at least 17,500 mph (28,000 km/h). This speed is called the Earth's orbital velocity. It is the speed a satellite needs to stay in orbit at a height of about 100 miles (160 km).

Satellite Orbits

Satellites are launched into a variety of orbits around the Earth. Some are launched in an equatorial orbit – one in which they travel over the Equator. Some are launched in a polar orbit – one in which they travel over the North and South Poles. Other satellites travel in an eccentric orbit. In this orbit, they travel in a looping path that takes them low over one side of the Earth and high over the other.

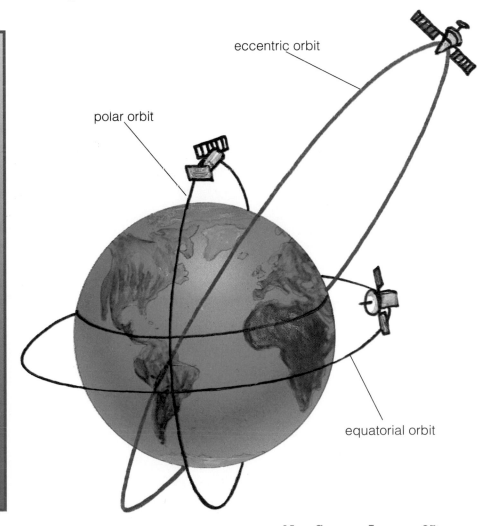

eccentric orbit

polar orbit

equatorial orbit

Orbital Period

When a satellite is circling in orbit at a height of 100 miles (160 km), it takes about 90 minutes to travel once around the Earth. This time is called its orbital period. In practice, satellites are launched into a much higher orbit because there is still enough air present 100 miles (160 km) up to slow them down. If they slow down, gravity pulls them back to Earth. The higher a satellite orbits, the longer is its orbital period. At a height of 1,000 miles (1,600 km), the period is about two hours. At a height of 10,000 miles (16,000 km), the period is over nine hours.

The 24–hour orbit

At a height of 22,300 miles (35,900 km), the orbital period of a satellite circling the Earth is 24 hours. This is the same time it takes the Earth to spin around once on its axis.

A satellite placed in this orbit over the Equator keeps pace with the Earth. It appears fixed, or stationary, in the sky. This kind of orbit is called geostationary, which means fixed in relation to the Earth.

The probe Ulysses, launched in 1990, followed a complicated trajectory. It went first to Jupiter. This giant planet's gravity speeded it up and flung it into an orbit that took it first beneath the south pole and then above the north pole of the Sun.

Jupiter's orbit

Sun

Jupiter

Earth

path of Ulysses

Escaping from Earth

By giving a spacecraft a speed of 17,500 mph (28,000 km/h), we can launch it into orbit as a satellite. It is in space but is still bound to the Earth by gravity.

To travel into outer space – to the Moon or the planets, a spacecraft must escape completely from gravity. To do this, it must be launched away from Earth at a very high speed: at least 25,000 mph (40,000 km/h). This speed is called the Earth's escape velocity.

We call spacecraft that escape gravity space probes. Lunar probes explore the Moon; planetary probes explore the planets.

Paths of probes

A space probe follows a curved trajectory, or path in space. Once it escapes from the Earth, it in effect becomes a miniature planet in orbit around the Sun and under the influence of the Sun's enormous gravity.

A probe is also affected by the gravity of other planets. This alters not only its trajectory but also its speed. Space scientists often take advantage of this to direct a probe from one planet to another. The technique is called the gravity-assist method. Voyager 2 used gravity-assist four times to travel to Neptune by way of Jupiter, Saturn, and Uranus (see pages 116–119).

The antenna at NASA's tracking station in Goldstone, California. It follows the trajectories of distant space probes by picking up their feeble radio signals.

When a satellite falls back to Earth, it smashes into the atmosphere at high speed. It breaks up into tiny pieces, which burn up like meteors.

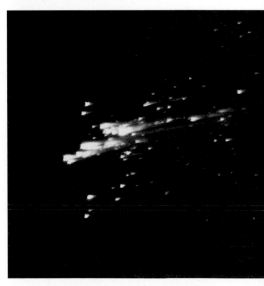

Launch Rockets

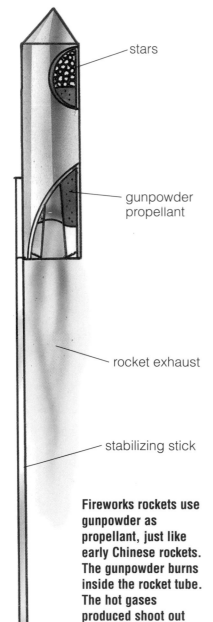

stars

gunpowder propellant

rocket exhaust

stabilizing stick

Fireworks rockets use gunpowder as propellant, just like early Chinese rockets. The gunpowder burns inside the rocket tube. The hot gases produced shoot out backward and propel the rocket forward.

As we have seen, to send satellites into orbit and probes into outer space, we must launch them from Earth at speeds of tens of thousands of miles an hour. Obviously, very powerful engines are needed to propel objects that fast.

Ordinary engines, such as gasoline and jet engines, are not powerful enough. They also have another disadvantage. They can't work in space because they need to take in oxygen from the air to burn their fuel.

We know of only one type of engine that is powerful enough for space travel. It is also the only engine that is able to work in airless space. It is the rocket. Rockets can work in space because they carry not only fuel, but also the oxygen to burn it.

Action/reaction

Rocket engines work by burning fuel in a chamber to make hot gases. The gases shoot backward at high speed out of a nozzle. As they shoot out backward, the engine is propelled forward. This follows from what is called the reaction principle.

The English scientist Isaac Newton first stated the principle in the 1600s as his third law of motion: "To every action there is an equal and opposite reaction."

In the rocket, the action is the force of the gases shooting backward. This action sets up a reaction in the opposite direction – a force forward that propels the rocket.

Rocket propellants

The Chinese invented the rocket about 1,000 years ago. They used gunpowder as the propelling substance, or propellant. Some space rockets use solid propellants today, but most use liquid propellants. The space shuttle, for example, uses solid propellants for its two boosters and liquid propellants for its main engines.

The design of a solid propellant rocket is quite simple. It consists of a tube, or casing, filled with propellant, with a nozzle at the end. The modern solid propellant consists of a kind of synthetic rubber mixed with powdered aluminum and ammonium perchlorate. The aluminum acts as fuel; the ammonium compound acts as the oxidizer, or the substance that provides oxygen.

Liquid propellant rockets

Rockets that burn liquid propellants are much more complicated in design. They have separate storage tanks to hold the fuel and oxidizer, along with pumps to pump them into the combustion chamber where they burn.

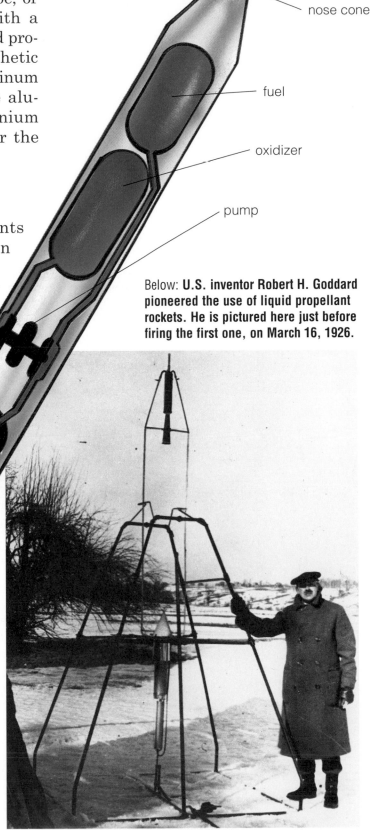

nose cone

fuel

oxidizer

pump

combustion chamber

Below: **U.S. inventor Robert H. Goddard pioneered the use of liquid propellant rockets. He is pictured here just before firing the first one, on March 16, 1926.**

The essential features of a liquid propellant rocket: fuel and oxidizer are pumped from separate tanks into the combustion chamber and ignited. The hot gases produced shoot backward out of the exhaust nozzle and propel the rocket forward.

Shuttle Thrust

Two of the best liquid propellants are liquid hydrogen for fuel and liquid oxygen for oxidizer. The space shuttle main engines use this combination, for example.

These engines are the most powerful engines for their size yet built. Each one weighs only about 3½ tons (3 tonnes), yet it produces a thrust (force forward) of more than 200 tons (180 tonnes).

Step by step

However, no matter what propellants we use and how big we build it, a single rocket can't lift itself into space. It is always too heavy to produce enough thrust.

Space scientists solve this problem by joining a number of rockets together, usually end to end. This arrangement is called a step rocket. Each separate rocket is called a stage.

Above: **A Delta rocket lifts off the launch pad at Cape Canaveral. Its boosters and main engines are firing together.**

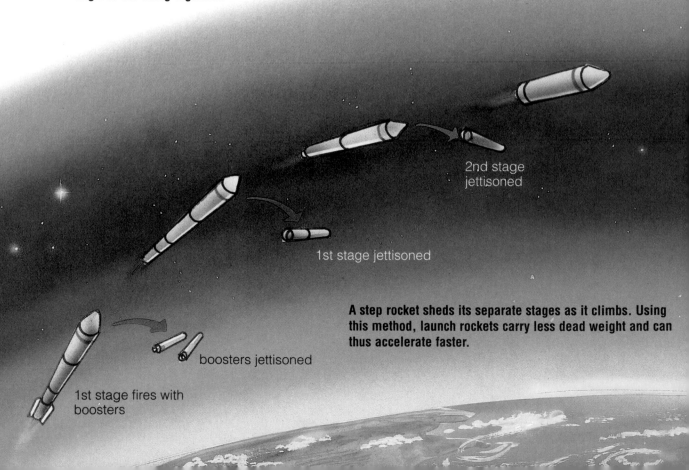

2nd stage jettisoned

1st stage jettisoned

boosters jettisoned

1st stage fires with boosters

A step rocket sheds its separate stages as it climbs. Using this method, launch rockets carry less dead weight and can thus accelerate faster.

The bottom rocket, or first stage, fires first and propels the ones above it high into the air. Then it falls away. The second stage fires and propels the now lighter rocket faster and higher. In turn, the second stage falls away, and the next stage fires, propelling the now even lighter rocket faster and higher still (see diagram below).

Launch vehicles

The step rockets used for space launchings are called launch vehicles. Many launch vehicles are made up of three main stages. The U.S. Delta launch vehicle has three main stages. It also has nine extra small rockets attached to the first stage. These are called strap-on boosters. They fire with the main engines during lift-off to provide extra power.

Launch vehicles can be enormous. The Delta, for example, stands about 115 feet (35 meters) high on the launch pad. Europe's Ariane 4 launcher stands up to about 190 feet (58 meters) high. Both would be dwarfed by the Saturn V launch vehicle, the biggest there has ever been (see right).

Ordinary launch rockets like the Delta and Ariane are called expendable launch vehicles (ELVs). They can be used only once. ELVs were the only kind of launch rockets until 1981. That year the first reusable launch vehicle came into use, the space shuttle orbiter Columbia (see page 92).

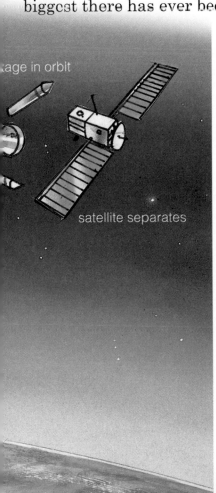

...age in orbit

satellite separates

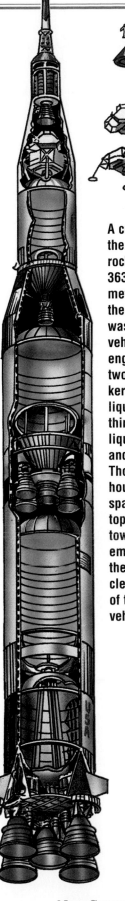

Apollo spacecraft

A cutaway view of the Saturn V rocket, which stood 363 feet (111 meters) high on the launch pad. It was a three-stage vehicle. The engines of the first two stages burned kerosene and liquid oxygen. The third stage burned liquid hydrogen and liquid oxygen. The nose cone housed the Apollo spacecraft. At the top was an escape tower, for use in an emergency, to pull the crew cabin clear from the rest of the launch vehicle.

Space Shuttle

At 7 a.m. on April 12, 1981, hundreds of thousands of people at the Kennedy Space Center in Florida witnessed the launch of a new kind of space vehicle. It was the space shuttle.

The part of the vehicle that carried the crew was the orbiter, named Columbia. It had wings and looked like a stubby airplane. It soared into the sky atop a huge tank, which carried fuel for its three rocket engines. Two booster rockets attached to the tank gave Columbia extra power for the lift-off. In turn, Columbia shed its booster rockets and tank, and then went into orbit.

For three days, the crew – veteran astronaut John Young and rookie Robert Crippen – thoroughly tested their craft. Then, after circling the Earth 36 times, they brought Columbia back to Earth. It glided to a perfect touchdown at Edwards Air Force Base near Los Angeles, California. The crew pronounced Columbia "a magnificent flying machine."

On November 12, Columbia went soaring into orbit once again. It was the first time that any space vehicle had gone into orbit more than once. A new era in space travel – the space shuttle era – had dawned.

Columbia went on to make a further three flights the next year. Then a new orbiter, Challenger, took over and in turn began flying back and forth between Earth and space.

○ When did the space shuttle first fly?
○ Who flew the first shuttle?
○ Why is the space shuttle different from other launch vehicles?
○ What is the Space Transportation System?
○ How is the space shuttle built?
○ How many space shuttles are there?
○ What is the purpose of the orbiter's fuel cells?
○ Why is the orbiter covered with tiles?

Opposite inset: **Columbia takes shape at the Rockwell International plant at Downey, California.**

Opposite:**The first shuttle flight begins on April 12, 1981. Columbia lifts off for the first of many times.**

Left: **Mounted on its launch platform, Columbia is rolled out to the launch pad at the Kennedy Space Center, ready for its first flight.**

Tank jettison.
About eight minutes into the flight,
the shuttle's main engines stop
firing, and the tank is jettisoned.

Booster separation.
About two minutes into the flight,
the boosters separate and
parachute back to Earth.

Shuttling into Orbit

Today, shuttle launches take place regularly up to eight or nine times a year. The repeat flights of the orbiters demonstrate the advantage of the shuttle over ordinary rocket launch vehicles. It is a reusable launch system. The orbiters are used over and over again. So are the booster rockets. Only the tank is not used again.

Another advantage of the shuttle is that it can carry a huge payload. In the payload bay, it can carry cargo up to nearly 60 feet (18 meters) long and 15 feet (4.6 meters) across. This means that it can carry several satellites at once, for example. Also, because the shuttle has a crew, they can check the satellites they have launched to make sure they are working properly. At other times, they can recover satellites from space and either repair them or bring them back to Earth.

Lift-off.
The shuttle's three main engines and the two
rocket boosters fire together to blast the shuttle off
the launch pad.

Mission operations.
The crew carry out mission activities, which might include launching spacecraft.

Orbit insertion.
The orbital maneuvering system (OMS) engines fire to boost the orbiter into orbit, typically at a height of about 200 miles (300 km).

Kennedy Spaceport

The only launch site for the shuttle is the Kennedy Space Center in Florida, often called the Kennedy Spaceport. .

At the Kennedy Space Center, the shuttle uses facilities built for the Apollo Moon landing missions. The launch stack of orbiter, boosters, and tank is put together in the mammoth Vehicle Assembly Building and rolled out to the launch pad on the huge crawler transporter built to carry the SaturnV/Apollo launch vehicles.

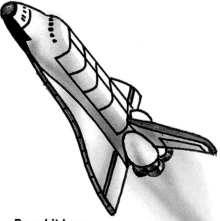

De-orbit burn.
With the orbiter now traveling tail first, the crew fires the OMS engines as a brake, and the orbiter comes out of orbit.

The shuttle fleet

The four orbiters in the shuttle fleet are Columbia, Discovery, Atlantis, and Endeavour. Discovery became operational in 1984, Atlantis in 1985, and Endeavour in 1991. Endeavour was built to replace Challenger, the second orbiter to be launched. Challenger exploded shortly after lift-off in January 1986, killing its crew of seven. As a result of the disaster, many changes were made in the shuttle and the way it is operated.

The first orbiter to take to the skies, however, was a flying test-bed. It was named Enterprise after the famous spacecraft in the Star Trek television series. It took part in gliding tests in the atmosphere, but never flew in space.

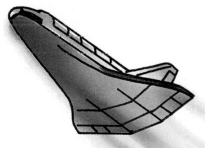

Re-entry.
The orbiter re-enters the atmosphere. The tiles covering the craft glow red hot because of friction with the air.

Runway touchdown.
Braked by the atmosphere, the orbiter glides in to land on a runway at a speed of about 220 mph (350 km/h).

Orbiter Systems

Here, we look at the construction of the orbiter and at some of the systems that allow it to operate as a launch vehicle. Details of the crew accommodation and other aspects of living in the orbiter in space are given later (see page 128).

The shuttle orbiter looks much like a plane, with wings and a tail. It has delta wings, in the shape of a triangle. The wings have hinged flaps called elevons at the rear. The tail has a rudder. The shuttle pilot uses elevons and the rudder to control the orbiter when gliding back through the atmosphere at the end of a mission.

The orbiter is built in much the same way as a plane. It is constructed mainly of lightweight aluminum alloys. The outer surface, however, is covered with insulating materials. This is to stop the heat

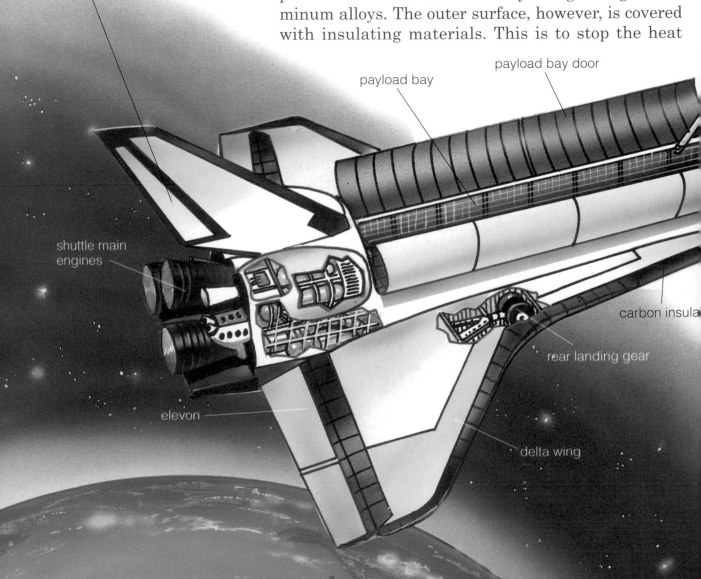

rudder

payload bay

payload bay door

shuttle main engines

carbon insula

rear landing gear

elevon

delta wing

produced during re-entry from getting to the aluminum and weakening it. The underside of the orbiter is covered with thick tiles made of silica. (silica is chemically the same as sand). The nose and wing edges are covered with a synthetic carbon material. These parts suffer the highest re-entry temperatures, up to 2,900°F (1,600°C).

Orbiter engines

The shuttle orbiter carries three main rocket engines, which burn liquid hydrogen and liquid oxygen. These propellants are fed to the engines from the external tank. The two solid rocket boosters (SRBs) that give added thrust at lift-off use solid propellants.

The orbiter is fitted with two smaller rockets, the orbital maneuvering system (OMS) engines. These fire to boost the orbiter into orbit and serve as a brake before re-entry. In addition, the orbiter has sets of small thruster jets in the nose and at the tail. They make up the reaction control system (RCS), which the orbiter uses to maneuver in space.

Fuel and power

The orbiter consumes a lot of power. It needs one form of power to swivel the engines and turn the rudder, for example. This is done by hydraulic power, the kind drivers use when they step on the brakes in a car. Hydraulic power on the shuttle is provided by a pump driven by small gas turbines.

The orbiter also needs electrical power to work the lights, instruments, computers, and other systems. The power comes from fuel cells. These are devices in which hydrogen and oxygen combine chemically to form water. Electricity is produced in the process.

The shuttle is controlled by computer most of the time because it is such a complicated vehicle. No human crew could keep track of all the systems or perform the hundreds of operations that need to be carried out all the time. In fact, the orbiter carries five computers that work together to process data. This arrangement allows for one or more computers to fail without putting the orbiter at risk.

satellite

remote manipulator system arm (robot arm)

pressurized crew cabin

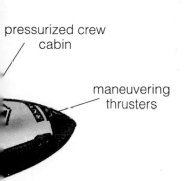

maneuvering thrusters

In orbit, the shuttle orbiter opens the doors of the payload bay. Some satellites are launched into space with the help of the robot arm, the shuttle's crane. Here are some data about the orbiter:
Length: 122 feet (37.2 meters)
Wingspan: 78 feet (23.8 meters)
Weight empty: 83 tons (75 tonnes)

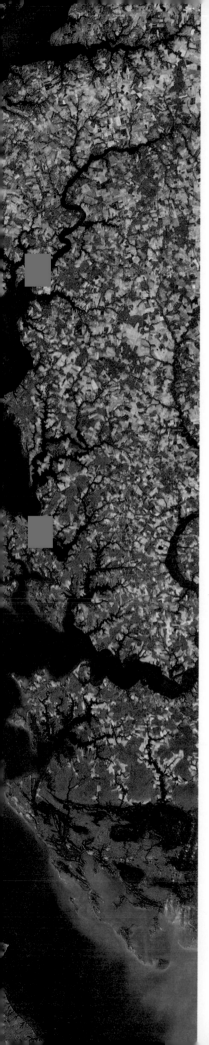

6 Spacecraft at Work

High above the Earth, hundreds of tiny artificial Moons travel silently in space. They are the spacecraft we call satellites. They circle endlessly around the Earth in orbit, bound to the Earth by gravity. Other spacecraft have escaped from Earth's gravity and are winging their way through interplanetary space. They are the spacecraft we call probes.

Satellites have become very useful in many fields. In particular, they have brought about a revolution in communications and made weather forecasting more accurate. Ships and aircraft now routinely use satellite navigation to guide them across the sea and through the air. Geographers use satellites to make better maps; prospectors use them to find hidden mineral deposits; and astronomers use them to get a clearer view of the Universe.

Space probes have given astronomers breathtaking close-up views of the planets. Probes have now visited all the planets except Pluto. Some probes are now billions of miles away, traveling out of the Solar System, bound for the stars.

The Earth-resources satellite Landsat returned this image of Washington D.C., Baltimore, and Chesapeake Bay. It clearly shows natural features and also reveals the influence of humans, in the patchwork of fields, networks of roads, and urban areas.

Satellite Anatomy

○ **How are satellites built?**
○ **What instruments do satellites carry?**
○ **Why do satellites carry a tape recorder?**
○ **What is telemetry?**

Spacecraft of all shapes and sizes circle around the Earth. They travel at very high speeds – tens of thousands of miles an hour, but they do not have to be smooth and streamlined like planes are. This is because they meet no air resistance out in space. They can take whatever shape is best for the job they have to do.

Structure and instruments

Satellites are built around a basic body structure, which carries the instruments, antennas, and other equipment. The body is built using lightweight alloys of aluminum and the even lighter metal beryllium. Carbon-fiber plastics may also be used.

The instruments a satellite carries depend on its work. They may include cameras, telescopes, and various kinds of sensors used to detect light and other rays, magnetism, and charged particles.

Below right: **An astronaut inspects Solar Max on the first satellite capture mission in 1984. He is riding on the shuttle's robot arm. Since then, astronauts have become skilled at recovering and repairing satellites in orbit.**

Below Left: **A TDRS tracking and relay satellite is ready for launch. Note that the technicians are wearing protective clothing to prevent the spacecraft from becoming contaminated.**

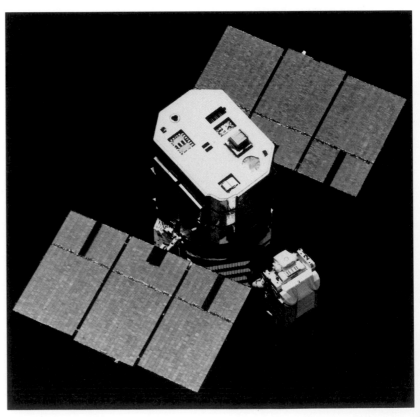

Communications

Measurements made by the instruments on board a satellite are radioed back to Earth through communications equipment. This includes a tape recorder and radio equipment. The tape recorder records the measurements until controllers on Earth instruct it to play them back over the radio. This process of getting information from satellites is called telemetry, a word meaning "measuring from a distance."

Antennas form an essential part of the communications equipment. Most satellites carry rod antennas for communications. Communications satellites have several dish antennas to send signals accurately to ground stations (see page 102). The dishes concentrate the signals into a directional beam.

Power

The instruments and other equipment on satellites work by electricity. Nearly all satellites use solar cells to produce the electricity. These cells harness the energy in Sunlight and convert it into electricity. They are made from thin slices of silicon, the same material used to make computer microchips.

solar panel unfolding

apogee motor

radio antennas

sensors

beam reflector

thermal blanket

A detailed look at an Intelsat V communications satellite. It is shown with its solar arrays unfolding. The apogee motor fires to position the satellite in the correct orbit. Sets of jet thrusters fire to keep the satellite on station – that is, in the correct position in orbit.

Everyday Satellites

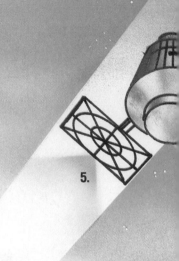

Among the most useful of all satellites orbiting the Earth are the ones that handle communications. When you pick up a telephone and dial a friend in Europe, your call travels out into space and back by way of a communications satellite (comsat) hovering over the Atlantic Ocean.

The satellite forms part of a network of comsats spaced around the world. All the satellites are in geostationary orbits, some 22,300 miles (35,900 km) high, and therefore appear to be fixed in the sky (see page 86). They hover above the Atlantic, Pacific, and Indian Oceans.

This international comsat network is operated by Intelsat, the International Telecommunications Satellite Organization. About 150 countries belong to Intelsat, which uses some of the most powerful comsats available. The Intelsat 6 satellites now in orbit can each handle up to 30,000 telephone conversations at the same time.

Many other comsats operate around the world, most of them in geostationary orbit. Telecommunications, news, and business organizations within the United States use a number of satellites for communications across the country. These satellites have such names as Westar, Galaxy, Satcom, and Telstar.

A Good Idea

The modern global communications network using satellites was first suggested by Arthur C. Clarke. He put forward the idea of relaying communications by way of satellites in geostationary orbit as early as 1945. The geostationary orbit is often called a Clarke orbit in his honor. Clarke is best known as a science fiction writer. The film classic *2001: A Space Odyssey*, is based on one of his stories.

Handling all traffic

Most comsats do more than just handle telephone calls. They also carry all other forms of electronic communications. They can relay fax messages, electronic mail, computer data, or television programs, for example.

Some comsats are leased by broadcasting companies to beam television programs directly into the home. The satellite TV programs can be picked up at home with a small dish antenna, commonly called a satellite dish. In some areas this gives viewers the choice of hundreds of television channels.

Ground stations

Signals are sent up to and received down from comsats at satellite ground stations. Hundreds of ground stations are now in operation throughout the world. They are linked with the normal telephone networks in the various countries in which they operate.

The most notable features of these stations are the large dish antennas. With this design, they can transmit signals up to satellites in a concentrated beam. Because each satellite hovers over the same spot on Earth, the antennas can stay permanently locked in position.

Making a transatlantic telephone call.

1. A caller in New York dials a friend in Paris, France.

2. Telephone signals travel by cable to a U.S. ground station.

3. At the ground station, the signals are converted into microwaves (short radio waves).

4. The microwave signals are beamed up to a comsat from a dish antenna.

5. The comsat receives the weak signals and amplifies (strengthens) them.

6. It then beams strong signals back down toward a ground station in France.

7. At the French ground station, a dish antenna picks up the signals. After they have again been amplified, the signals are fed into the French telephone network.

8. Finally, the signals reach the telephone of the person being called. All this has happened in a fraction of a second.

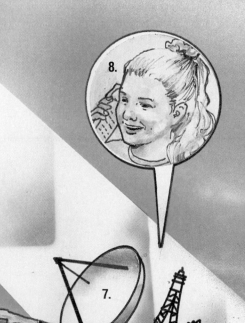

Watching the Weather

This NOAA weather satellite circles the Earth over the North and South Poles. It measures about 14 feet (4.2 meters) long and weighs nearly 2 tons (1.8 tonnes).

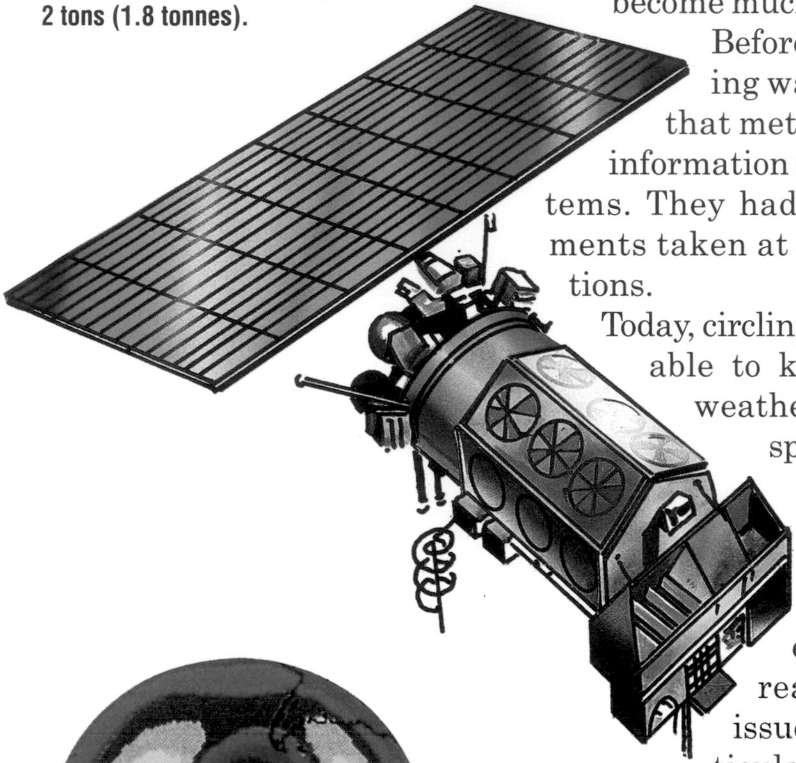

Meteorology – the study of the weather – is another field that has been revolutionized by space technology. The result has been that weather forecasting has become much more accurate.

Before the Space Age began, forecasting was unreliable. The problem was that meteorologists couldn't get enough information about approaching weather systems. They had to rely on weather measurements taken at only a handful of weather stations.

Today, circling in space, weather satellites are able to keep continuous watch on the weather all over the world. They can spot when and where weather systems are born and follow them as they develop, hour by hour.

Armed with this information, meteorologists can calculate exactly when the systems will reach particular regions, and issue accurate forecasts. This is particularly valuable in the case of severe storms and hurricanes. Knowing that such storms are coming, meteorologists can warn people in their path and save lives.

Weather satellites carry cameras to take pictures of clouds. They also have instruments sensitive to infrared light. This means that they can take pictures at night. They measure temperatures on the ground and at different levels in the atmosphere. They also measure the amount of moisture in the air.

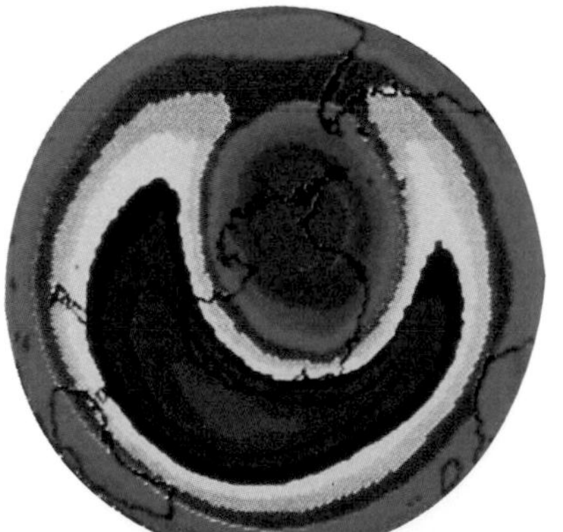

Above: **The Nimbus 7 environmental satellite was first to report the ozone hole – a marked thinning of the ozone layer around the Earth at certain times of the year. The ozone layer helps protect us from harmful rays of the Sun. The picture shows the very low concentration of ozone (mauve) over the South Pole in winter.**

NOAA and GOES

Two series of satellites keep a weather eye on the Americas. The NOAA series uses satellites that operate about 500 miles (800 km) high in an orbit that takes them over the Poles. They view the weather over the whole globe twice a day. NOAA stands for the National Oceanic and Atmospheric Administration, the U.S. organization that operates the satellites.

The other satellites that report on American weather are GOES (Geostationary Observational Environmental Satellites). They are located in geostationary (fixed) orbit over the Atlantic and Pacific Oceans. They send back images of a full disk of the Earth, showing North and South America, about every half hour.

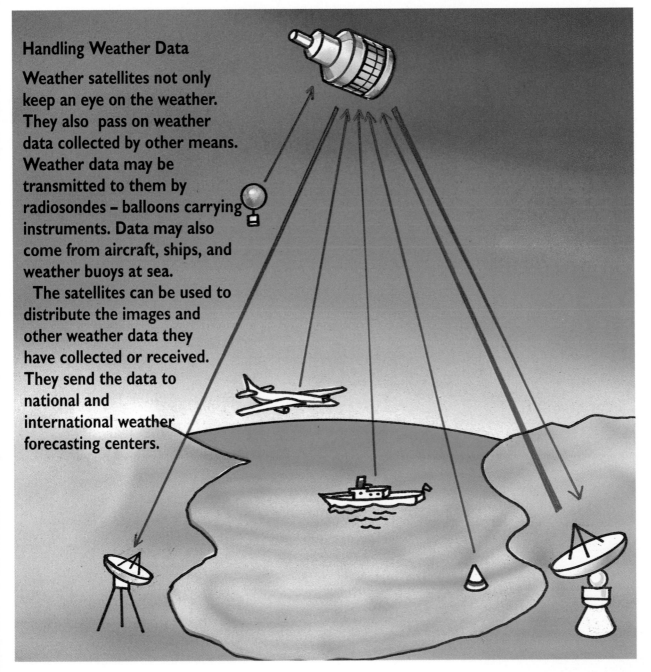

Handling Weather Data

Weather satellites not only keep an eye on the weather. They also pass on weather data collected by other means. Weather data may be transmitted to them by radiosondes – balloons carrying instruments. Data may also come from aircraft, ships, and weather buoys at sea.

The satellites can be used to distribute the images and other weather data they have collected or received. They send the data to national and international weather forecasting centers.

Surveying Earth's Resources

Earth resources satellites scan the surface of the Earth in narrow bands. The U.S. Landsat (below) scans a single band 115 miles (185 km) across. The French SPOT (above) makes a double scan covering a similar width.

Another kind of satellite looks at the Earth for a different purpose. It is called an Earth resources satellite because it gives us information about the Earth's resources, such as the land, the oceans, forests, and mineral deposits.

Earth resources satellites are valuable to all kinds of people in business, science, and industry. They greatly benefit such workers as map makers, town planners, geologists, foresters, and farmers. From images the satellites send back, farmers, for example, can spot the difference between healthy and diseased crops. Geologists can pinpoint where there may be valuable new mineral deposits. Town planners can see quickly where new building developments are taking place.

Scanning the landscape

Earth resources satellites do not take photographs of the surface. Instead, they produce electronic signals that computers turn into images. They view the surface with a device called a scanner.

The United States launched two Earth resources satellites of this design, named Landsat 4 and 5. Including the solar panels, the spacecraft measures about 14 feet (4 meters) long. The Landsats have mapped the whole of the Earth's surface in great detail. They scan the surface not only at visible wavelengths (colors) of light, but also at invisible wavelengths, such as infrared.

This moves from side to side, looking at the surface strip by strip. From the signals the scanner sends back, an image of the surface is built up strip by strip. The picture on a television screen is built up in a similar way.

The scanner does not see in ordinary white light. Instead, it sees in light of different colors. This helps show up different kinds of features on the Earth's surface.

Computer colors

The images Earth resources satellites send back look very different from ordinary colored photographs of the same regions. Their colors are false, or not true to life.

The computers that produce the images from the satellite data can display them in a wide range of false colors. Usually, the colors are chosen so as to show up special surface features, such as diseased crops in a field.

San Francisco Bay pictured by Landsat 4. Many details of the landscape can be seen, even the bridges across the bay.

Looking at the Universe

○ **Why can astronomers see the Universe better with space telescopes?**
○ **What invisible rays from space does the atmosphere block?**
○ **How big is the Hubble Space Telescope?**
○ **How does it send back pictures?**

For the astronomer, satellites are very useful, carrying telescopes and other instruments above the Earth's atmosphere. To the astronomer on Earth, the atmosphere acts like a dirty window because it is full of dust and moisture. It dims and distorts the light coming in from the heavenly bodies. Out in space, the view of the Universe is crystal clear.

The blocking atmosphere

The Earth's atmosphere is a nuisance to astronomers for another reason. It blocks out other radiation (rays) that the heavenly bodies give out.

Stars and galaxies give out energy not only as visible light rays, but also as invisible gamma rays, X-rays, ultraviolet rays, and infrared rays. The atmosphere absorbs all or most of these other rays and prevents them from reaching telescopes on the ground.

Studying all rays

Thanks to satellites, astronomers can now study all the rays that heavenly bodies give out. By doing so, they have gained a better understanding about what these bodies and our Universe are like. Satellites such as Einstein (which studied X-rays), IRAS (infrared rays), COBE (microwaves), Compton (gamma rays), and Rosat (X-rays) have made some of the most exciting discoveries in astronomy in recent years.

For example:

*Einstein discovered mysterious machinegun-like bursts of X-rays coming from the heavens.

Below: **The Hubble Space Telescope undergoes a final check before launch.**

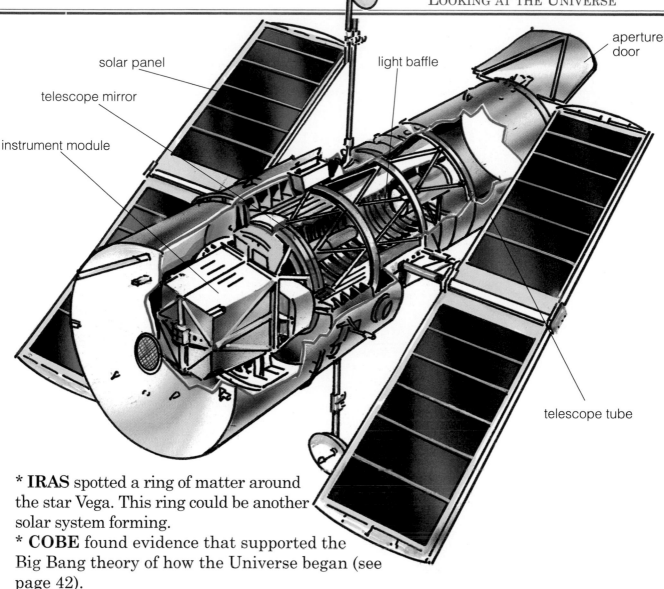

solar panel

telescope mirror

instrument module

light baffle

aperture door

telescope tube

* **IRAS** spotted a ring of matter around the star Vega. This ring could be another solar system forming.

* **COBE** found evidence that supported the Big Bang theory of how the Universe began (see page 42).

* **Compton** discovered intense gamma rays coming from a quasar seven billion light-years away — halfway across the known Universe.

* **Rosat** found huge masses of dark matter, never detected before.

Many exciting discoveries in visible ligh are also being made from spacet by the Hubble Space Telescope (HST). For example, it has peered into the center of distant galaxies and found evidence of massive black holes. In general it is giving astronomers their clearest views yet of the Universe. When the HST was first launched (1990), its mirrors were found to be faulty, which ruined the images it took. Finally in 1993, shuttle astronauts repaired the HST in orbit, and it is now producing excellent images.

The Hubble Space Telescope (HST) is large and heavy. It measures 42 feet (13 meters) long and weighs 12 tons (11 tonnes). It gathers the light from heavenly bodies with a main mirror 95 inches (2.4 meters) across. A second mirror reflects the light through a hole in the main mirror. The light is then directed to cameras and other instruments. Images from the cameras are converted into electronic signals and beamed to Earth from the HST's antennas. Computers convert the signals into visible pictures. This takes place at the Space Telescope Institute, located in Baltimore, Maryland.

Probing Outer Space

○ **What is the most important difference between a probe and a satellite?**
○ **What is the advantage of a dish antenna?**
○ **How are probes powered?**
○ **What is an RTG?**

The spacecraft we call satellites travel in space, but only in what we might call near space, the space around the Earth. They are still bound to the Earth by gravity.

The spacecraft we call space probes, however, escape from the clutches of Earth's gravity and travel into outer space, the space in which the planets travel.

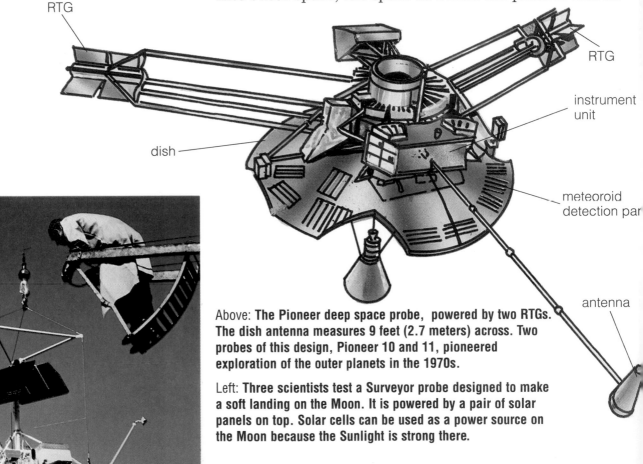

RTG

RTG

dish

instrument unit

meteoroid detection par

antenna

Above: **The Pioneer deep space probe, powered by two RTGs. The dish antenna measures 9 feet (2.7 meters) across. Two probes of this design, Pioneer 10 and 11, pioneered exploration of the outer planets in the 1970s.**

Left: **Three scientists test a Surveyor probe designed to make a soft landing on the Moon. It is powered by a pair of solar panels on top. Solar cells can be used as a power source on the Moon because the Sunlight is strong there.**

To do this, they must be launched away from Earth at much higher speeds than satellites by more powerful launch rockets (see page 88–89).

Anatomy of probes

In general, probes are built in much the same way as satellites (see page 100). They are constructed from light alloys and are equipped with a variety of instruments, including cameras, radiation and particle detectors, and magnetometers.

The communication equipment on probes, however, is more powerful, so that signals can be transmitted and received over great distances. It includes an antenna with a large dish reflector. The dish provides a larger area to collect the faint signals sent from Earth. When transmitting, the dish helps beam signals back to Earth in the right direction.

This picture shows a Voyager probe speeding past Saturn, four years after it was launched from Earth and more than 18 months after visiting Jupiter.

Nuclear power

Probes sent to the Moon and the nearer planets – Mercury, Venus, and Mars – are powered by solar cells, like satellites. However, solar cells can't be used on probes sent to Jupiter and the other outer planets. This is because Sunlight in the outer Solar System is too weak, and solar cells could not produce enough electricity.

Probes venturing far from the Sun are therefore equipped with a nuclear power source. They have what are called RTGs, or radioisotope thermoelectric generators. RTGs contain plutonium, a radioactive substance (radioisotope), that gives off radiation and heat. Devices called thermocouples convert the heat into electricity.

Looking at Neighbors

○ **Which probes investigated the Moon?**
○ **What did Mariner 10 discover about Mercury?**
○ **What does gravity-assist mean?**
○ **Why is radar used to look at Venus?**
○ **Did the Viking probes find any life on Mars?**

As could be expected, the first probes were aimed at the Moon, our nearest neighbor in space. Russia achieved success first in January 1959 with a near fly-by by Luna 1.

The United States did not launch a successful lunar probe until July 1964. Named Ranger 7, it sent back thousands of high-quality pictures of the Moon's surface before crash landing as planned. Two other successful Ranger missions followed.

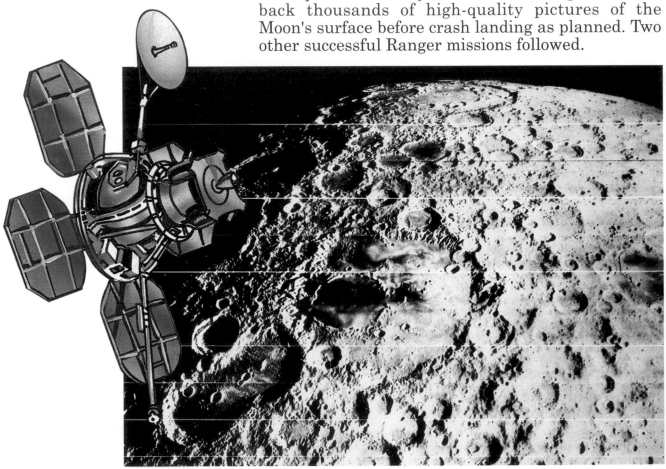

Inset: **Five Lunar Orbiters of this design mapped nearly the whole surface of the Moon from orbit in 1966 and 1967.**

Above right: **A Lunar Orbiter picture of the Moon. The probe scanned the surface in narrow strips, which were put together to form a larger picture.**

Then in 1966, NASA launched the first in a series of Surveyor and Lunar Orbiter probes to prepare the way for the Apollo Moon landing missions (see page 60). The Surveyors were designed to make a soft landing on the surface. The Lunar Orbiters photographed the Moon from orbit, looking closely at possible Moon landing sites.

Moonwalker

The Russians also launched successful orbiting and landing probes. Among them were the Luna 16 and 17 probes that landed in 1970. Luna 16 was a sample and return mission: the probe dug up a sample of Moon soil and returned it to Earth. Luna 17 delivered a wheeled vehicle, named Lunokhod, meaning "moonwalker." It trundled slowly over the surface, controlled by scientists on Earth looking through the vehicle's television camera eyes.

Off to the planets

Both the United States and Russia began trying to launch probes to the planets in 1960. The United States was first to succeed with the probe Mariner 2, sent to Venus. It passed within 22,000 miles (35,000 km) of the planet. It reported that the surface of Venus was unbelievably hot, with a temperature of more than 800°F (425°C). The atmosphere was very dense, and its pressure was at least 20 times the atmospheric pressure on Earth. Russian Venera probes also targeted Venus, with Venera 4 in 1967 parachuting a capsule into the atmosphere.

Mariner to Mercury

A later U.S. probe to Venus, Mariner 10, had a dual mission. After photographing Venus in 1973, it sped on to Mercury and made three passes over the planet. It revealed that Mercury is as hot as Venus and highly cratered, with a landscape similar to that of the Moon.

Right: **Hundreds of craters, large and small, cover Mercury's Sun-baked surface.**

Mariner 10, the first probe to visit two planets, Mercury and Venus, in 1973 and 1974.

Under the Clouds

Inset: **Magellan, launched from the space shuttle in 1989, went into orbit around Venus in 1990.**

Above right: **Magellan's radar view of Venus reveals a highly complex surface very different from that of Earth or any other planet.**

Venus is permanently covered in thick clouds, which means that the surface can't be seen from orbit. The first glimpse of the surface came in 1975, when the Russian probes Venera 9 and 10 landed instrument capsules on Venus. They sent back close-up pictures of the surface.

Three years later, the U.S. Pioneer Venus Orbiter gave us the first broad view of the surface. It scanned

View of the Martian surface from the Viking 1 lander. The digging scoop of the lander can be seen on the right. The landscape is strewn with rocks and is a red-orange color, like rust.

the planet with radar, which can see through clouds. In 1990, Magellan also used radar to map the whole surface of Venus for the first time.

The Red Planet

The U.S. probe Mariner 4 was first to encounter Mars, in 1965. It sent back a few low-quality pictures, showing a heavily cratered landscape. They were the first pictures of another planet ever seen on Earth.

Mariner 4's journey was the first in a string of successful Mars encounters by U.S. probes. The peak of achievement was reached in 1976, when two Viking probes went into orbit around the planet. They released landing craft that dropped down to the surface.

Viking invasion

The Viking 1 lander set down on Mars in a region called Chryse; Viking 2 in Utopia. Both are relatively flat plains. The equipment on the landers included cameras, weather instruments, and a miniature laboratory with an oven. The landers also had a robot arm with a scoop to dig up the soil and deliver it to the laboratory.

The chief purpose of the laboratory was to test the soil for signs of life. When the tests were carried out, some strong reactions occurred. Scientists first thought that these reactions indicated that organic matter was present, but they now believe that the reactions were caused by peculiar chemistry.

The United States resumed missions to Mars with the launch of the Mars Observer in 1992. Unfortunately, contact was lost with the probe the following year, just before it was due to go into orbit. It was the first of a series of missions that will lead some time in the 21st century to human exploration of the Red Planet.

Right: **Viking landing operations:**
1. Viking orbiter releases capsule. 2. Parachute opens. 3. Protective aeroshell jettisoned. 4. Rocket braking. 5. Lander sets down on surface.

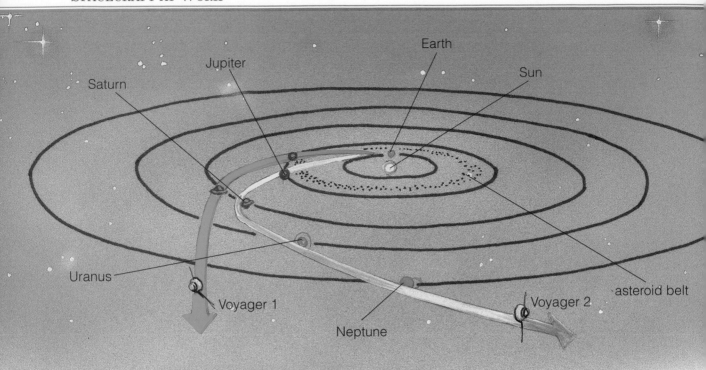

This diagram shows the paths of the two Voyager probes through the Solar System. They are both now speeding toward interstellar space – the space between the stars.

Visiting Distant Worlds

After sending successful missions to Mars, NASA turned its attention to Jupiter, the next planet out in the Solar System. Jupiter is the biggest of the four giant planets, made up mostly of gas. The others are Saturn, Uranus, and Neptune.

Sending a probe to Jupiter would present a great challenge because of the distances involved. It would have to travel hundreds of millions of miles to reach its target. Communicating with a probe over such distances would also be a challenge.

There was another major problem. To reach Jupiter, a probe would have to travel through the asteroid belt. This is a ring of mini-planets, composed of rocky chunks of up to about 600 miles (1,000 km) across.

Pioneering probes

NASA launched the first probe, named Pioneer 10, toward Jupiter in March 1972. If all went well, it

○ **Why does the asteroid belt pose a problem to probes?**
○ **Which planets did Pioneer 10 and 11 visit?**
○ **What discoveries did the Voyagers make?**
○ **Why was Voyager 2 able to make a grand tour of four planets?**
○ **What is Galileo's mission?**

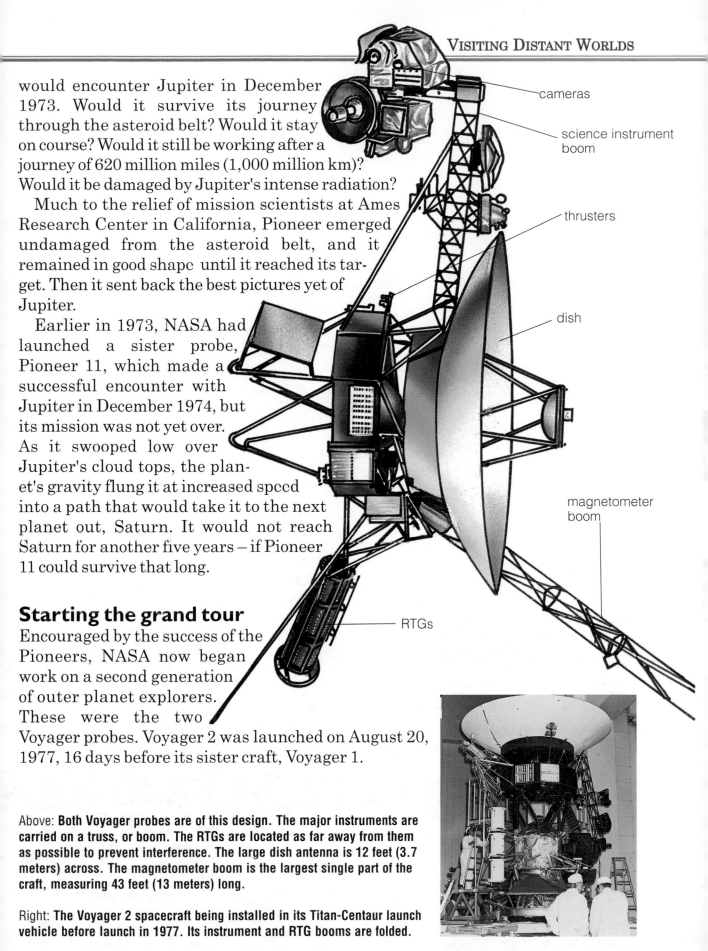

would encounter Jupiter in December 1973. Would it survive its journey through the asteroid belt? Would it stay on course? Would it still be working after a journey of 620 million miles (1,000 million km)? Would it be damaged by Jupiter's intense radiation?

Much to the relief of mission scientists at Ames Research Center in California, Pioneer emerged undamaged from the asteroid belt, and it remained in good shape until it reached its target. Then it sent back the best pictures yet of Jupiter.

Earlier in 1973, NASA had launched a sister probe, Pioneer 11, which made a successful encounter with Jupiter in December 1974, but its mission was not yet over. As it swooped low over Jupiter's cloud tops, the planet's gravity flung it at increased speed into a path that would take it to the next planet out, Saturn. It would not reach Saturn for another five years – if Pioneer 11 could survive that long.

cameras

science instrument boom

thrusters

dish

magnetometer boom

RTGs

Starting the grand tour

Encouraged by the success of the Pioneers, NASA now began work on a second generation of outer planet explorers. These were the two Voyager probes. Voyager 2 was launched on August 20, 1977, 16 days before its sister craft, Voyager 1.

Above: **Both Voyager probes are of this design. The major instruments are carried on a truss, or boom. The RTGs are located as far away from them as possible to prevent interference. The large dish antenna is 12 feet (3.7 meters) across. The magnetometer boom is the largest single part of the craft, measuring 43 feet (13 meters) long.**

Right: **The Voyager 2 spacecraft being installed in its Titan-Centaur launch vehicle before launch in 1977. Its instrument and RTG booms are folded.**

Ambitious Plans

Mission controllers at the Jet Propulsion Laboratory in Pasadena, California, planned for Voyager 1 to visit Jupiter and Saturn. Their plans for Voyager 2 were much more ambitious, nothing less than a grand tour of the outer planets The tour would take Voyager 2 beyond Jupiter and Saturn to Uranus and Neptune on a mission lasting 12 years.

A grand tour of the four planets would be possible because of the way they would be aligned in space over the 12-year period. Such an alignment comes about only once every 175 years.

A flood of discoveries

Voyager 1 arrived first at Jupiter, approaching closest in March 1979.

Left: **Jupiter's large Moon Io, the most colorful Moon in the whole Solar System. Mission scientists nicknamed it the pizza Moon. (Voyager 1 image)**

Below: **Linda Morabito, who first spotted volcanoes erupting on Io. She is a Voyager mission specialist at the Jet Propulsion Laboratory, Pasadena.**

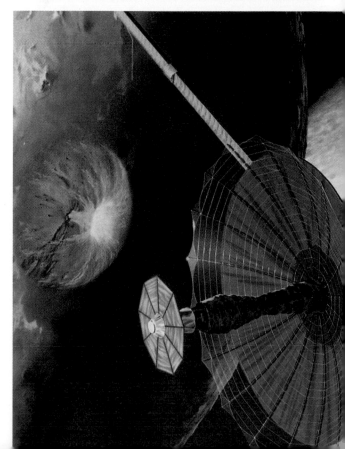

Voyager 2 followed four months later. Together, they sent back thousands of images of the vividly colored planet and its largest Moons and made many new discoveries. For example, they discovered three new Moons and found that Jupiter has a faint ring around it. They also spied volcanoes erupting on the Moon Io.

Both Voyagers next encountered the glorious ringed planet Saturn-Voyager 1 in November 1980, Voyager 2 in August 1981. They were not the first probes to visit the planet, however. Pioneer 11 got there first, in August 1979, spotting a new ring and a new Moon.

In their turn, the Voyagers discovered more new rings and more new Moons. They showed that the large rings visible from Earth are made up of thousands of separate ringlets.

Above: **Voyager 2 leaves Earth aboard its Titan-Centaur rocket carrier from Cape Canaveral on August 20, 1977.**

Below: **Saturn's rings and its northern hemisphere were pictured by Voyager 2 as it approached the planet. Voyager 2 was 27,000,000 miles (43,000,000 km) from Saturn when it took this false color photograph.**

Left: **Galileo is the spacecraft to encounter Jupiter in 1995. It will drop a probe into the atmosphere to report on conditions there. It will also report on conditions on Jupiter's Moons.**

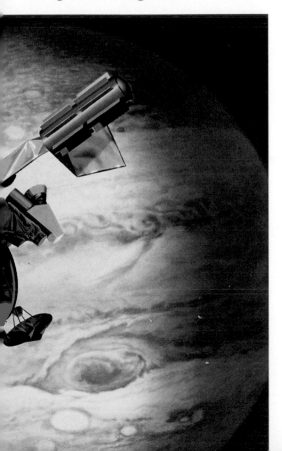

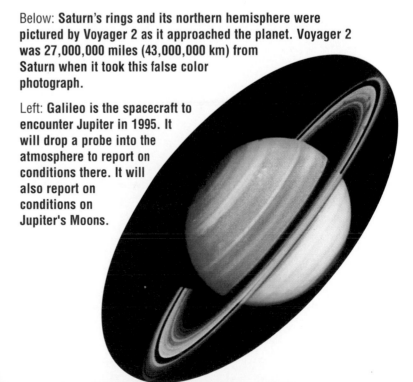

On to New Worlds

What a Putt!

Guiding Voyager 2 to an on-target encounter with Neptune, over a distance of nearly 4.5 billion miles (7 billion km), is equivalent to a golfer sinking a putt from a distance of 3,000 miles (5,000 km)!

After visiting Saturn, Voyager 1's encounter days were over and it began its long journey out of the Solar System. Voyager 2, however, still had new worlds to conquer.

After leaving Saturn, Voyager 2 set course for Uranus, arriving there in January 1986. During the five-year journey, mission scientists reprogrammed Voyager's computers to improve the process by which it took images and transmitted image data back to Earth.

They also enlarged the dish antennas of their tracking stations in the Deep Space Network. They needed bigger antennas to pick up the very weak signals Voyager 2 transmitted during encounter. At this time it was nearly 2 billion miles (3 billion km) away from Earth. Its radio waves took 2¾ hours to make the journey.

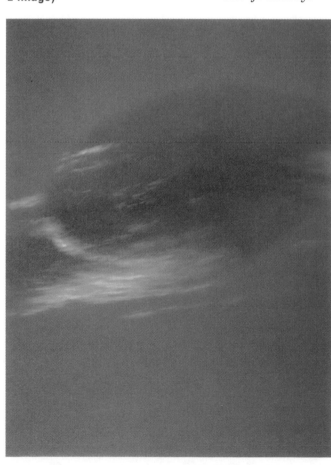

Below: **Neptune's Great Dark Spot, flecked with white clouds. It is probably a storm center. (Voyager 2 image)**

The final encounter

After its third successful encounter, with Uranus, Voyager 2 had to travel for another 3½ years before it encountered its last target planet, Neptune. As before, mission scientists reprogrammed the computers and improved communications equipment.

Precisely on target and precisely on time on August 20, 1989, Voyager 2 flew by Neptune. It skimmed past only about 3,000 miles (5,000 km) from the cloud tops. This was Voyager 2's closest encounter with a planet in its 12-year journey of discovery.

The images of Neptune that Voyager 2 sent were of remarkably good quality, considering how far away it was at the time – nearly 2,750 million miles (4,400 million km).

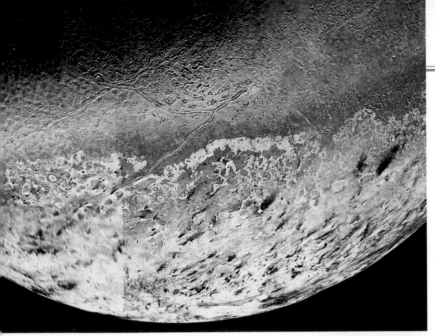

Left: **The south pole of Triton is covered with pinkish snow. It is probably made up of frozen methane and nitrogen. The dark streaks show where volcanoes have erupted. (Voyager 2 image)**

Deep-frozen Triton

Voyager 2 sped past Neptune and headed toward the planet's largest Moon, Triton. It showed this Moon to be an astonishing body. The surface is scarred with faults and craters. Parts of it are covered in what appears to be pinkish snow.

Also, Triton has volcanoes, which give out nitrogen vapor and liquid nitrogen when they erupt. They do not give out red hot molten rock like volcanoes on Earth because the Moon is too cold (–390°F, –236°C). In fact, Triton is the coldest body we know of in the whole Solar System.

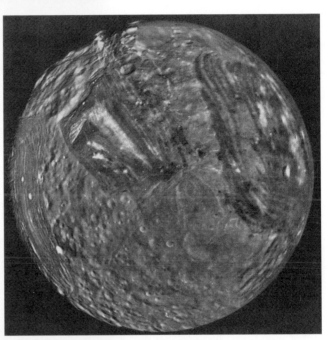

Above: **The Uranus Moon Miranda, which has most peculiar markings on its surface. (Voyager 2 image)**

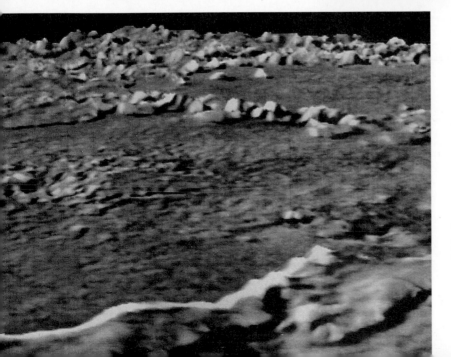

Left: **This is one of the many ice-filled craters Voyager 2 spied on Triton.**

Hello Out There!

Pioneer 10 and 11 and the two Voyager probes are now on their way out of the Solar System. They will then begin traveling through interstellar space – the space between the stars. Interstellar space is so vast that it will be tens of thousands of years before they get close to another star.

Each of the four probes is headed in a different direction. Pioneer 10 is headed toward the constellation Taurus (the Bull), Pioneer 11 toward Sagittarius (the Archer), Voyager 1 toward Camelopardalis (the Giraffe), and Voyager 2 toward Andromeda.

Pictures and sounds of Earth

It is just possible that, in many thousands of years, one of these four space probes will wander into another solar system and be found by intelligent alien beings.

Just in case this does happen, the probes carry ingenious messages for aliens. The messages tell them where the probes came from and who sent them. They were thought up by the well-known U.S. astronomer Carl Sagan.

Above: **The record, *Sounds of Earth*, is carried by the Voyager probes. It carries greetings in 60 languages from different peoples, along with sounds of nature and the man-made world. It also carries photographs of our world, recorded in code.**

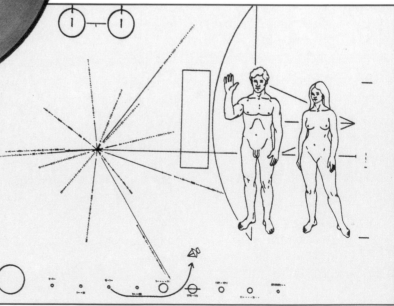

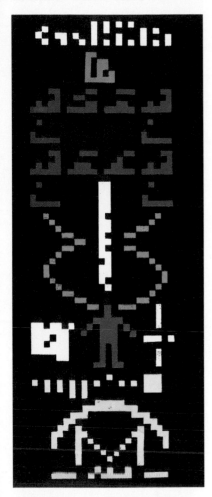

Above: **This is a picture version of the message beamed from the Arecibo radio telescope in 1974. Easy to recognize are the spiral shape of DNA (blue), the human figure (red), and the telescope itself (green).**

Left: **This plaque is carried by the Pioneer 10 and 11 space probes. It shows a naked man and woman drawn to the same scale as the spacecraft in the background. The starburst of lines gives the location of the Sun among the stars. The diagram at the bottom shows which planet in our Solar System the spacecraft came from.**

The Pioneer probes carry a picture message on a plaque. The Voyager probes go one better and carry a record disc, called *Sounds of Earth*, which includes pictures as well as sounds from Earth. Instructions on how to play the disc are given on the record cover.

Message from Arecibo

Intelligent aliens on other worlds could also find out about life on Earth from the radio transmissions that come from our planet. Because radio waves travel at the speed of light, they could, if they were strong enough, reach nearby stars in a matter of years.

With this in mind, scientists in 1974 used the radio telescope at Arecibo in Puerto Rico to beam a message into the heavens. The message tells about life on Earth, including the nature of DNA, the human body, and Earth's population.

As well as sending messages to other worlds, scientists are hoping to receive messages from them. This is the aim of what is called SETI, the search for extraterrestrial intelligence. SETI scientists study signals from the heavens picked up by radio telescopes. They look for any artificial pattern in the signals that might be a coded message from another civilization. So far they have had no success.

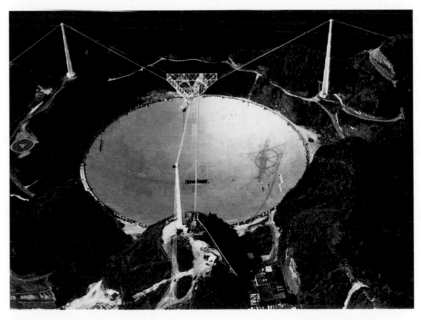

Above: **The Arecibo radio telescope in Puerto Rico. Its dish measures 1,000 feet (305 meters) across.**

7 Humans in Space

A momentous event in the history of the human race took place on April 12, 1961. On that day a Russian pilot, Yuri Gagarin, became the first human being to travel in space. John Glenn became the first American in orbit on February 20, 1962. Gagarin was the first cosmonaut ("sailor in the Universe"); Glenn, the first astronaut ("star sailor").

Glenn's flight was the first of four one-man missions into orbit in Project Mercury, the program to put Americans in space. It was the first stage of a three-stage program to put U.S. astronauts on the Moon by the end of the 1960s. The second stage in the program was Project Gemini, which began in 1965. The Gemini spacecraft carried a crew of two.

On 12 successful missions, Gemini astronauts gained experience of long space flights and of spacewalking. They also rehearsed techniques that would be needed for the next push into the Universe. This was Project Apollo to land astronauts on the Moon.

In December 1968, astronauts made the first round trip to the Moon in the Apollo 8 spacecraft, but didn't land. Two Apollo 11 astronauts made the first human footprints in the lunar soil on July 20, 1969. Five more Moon landings followed, each more spectacular than the one before. Human beings were beginning to conquer space, often called the last great frontier.

Since then, humankind has continued to push back that frontier, with the launch of the space shuttle and space stations, ever more daring spacewalks, and longer and longer space flights.

Astronauts on shuttle mission 51A celebrate the recovery of two satellites that have been stranded in orbit for nine months. Daring missions like this demonstrate how astronauts can work well in the space environment.

Step by Step

This series of photographs features some of the astronauts, both American and Russian, who helped pioneer the human exploration of space. It spans exactly the first two decades of human space flight, from Yuri Gagarin's first orbit of the Earth to Columbia's first flight, which ushered in the space shuttle era.

1961
Russian cosmonaut Yuri Gagarin was the first man in space. He soared into orbit on April 12, 1961, in the space capsule Vostok 1. On his single orbit, he reached a height of more than 200 miles (320 km) above the Earth. Tragically, he was killed in a plane crash seven years later.

1961
Alan Shepard became the first American in space on May 5, 1961. He flew briefly into space while traveling in a sub-orbital trajectory in the Mercury capsule Freedom 7. He is seen here being congratulated by President John F. Kennedy, who would shortly announce the Apollo program to put an American on the Moon.

1962
John Glenn climbs into his Mercury capsule, Friendship 7, on February 20, 1962. Hours later, he is circling the Earth in space, becoming the first American in orbit. His three-orbit flight lasts nearly five hours.

1963
Russian cosmonaut Valentina Tereshkova became the first woman to fly in space on March 6, 1963. She remained in orbit in a Vostok capsule for nearly three days. No other woman ventured into space for 19 years.

1965
Edward White makes the first American spacewalk on June 3, 1965, just a few weeks after the first ever spacewalk by Russian cosmonaut Alexei Leonov. It was one of the early highlights of the Gemini project. White was killed in January 1967 while training for the first Apollo Moon landing mission.

1969
It is July 20, 1969. Human beings from planet Earth are walking on another world, the Moon. They are the Apollo 11 astronauts Neil Armstrong and Edwin Aldrin. Ten other Apollo astronauts followed them to plant their footprints in the lunar soil.

1981
On April 12, 1981, the orbiter Columbia pioneered the modern era of space transportation by space shuttle. It was 20 years to the day after the first human went into space. Here, commander John Young catches up on some paperwork during the first shuttle mission, STS-1. This was Young's record fifth trip into space, having flown previously on two Gemini and two Apollo missions.

1975
On July 17, 1975, U.S. astronauts and Russian cosmonauts take part in the first international space link-up, the Apollo Soyuz Test Project (ASTP). Pictured in the hatch between the Soyuz spacecraft and the docking module on Apollo are the two flight commanders: Thomas Stafford and Alexei Leonov.

Astronauts in Training

○ **What kinds of astronauts are mission specialists and payload specialists?**
○ **How do astronauts train for weightlessness?**
○ **What is a simulator?**

All the early astronauts were highly skilled and highly experienced test pilots, used to flying superfast jet planes. At the start of the space program, pilot-astronauts were needed to test-fly entirely new kinds of craft being developed to travel in space. Today, pilot-astronauts form just one category of astronaut. In the U.S. space program, the primary job of pilot-astronauts is to fly the space shuttle.

Two other categories of astronaut fly on shuttle missions: mission specialists and payload specialists. Mission specialists are full-time astronauts who are concerned with mission operations, such as conducting experiments and launching satellites. They do not need to know how to fly the shuttle. Most are well-qualified scientists and engineers.

Payload specialists are not full-time astronauts. They fly on a mission to carry out particular experiments or supervise certain payload operations for

Below right: **Astronauts float weightless for a few minutes in a diving plane. This gives them an idea of what to expect when they get into space.**

Below: **Divers help astronauts practice for space walking in a huge water tank. The astronauts wear suits similar to spacesuits, which are weighted so that they neither rise nor sink.**

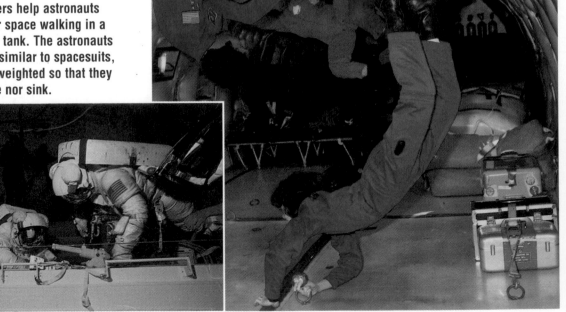

which they have specialized knowledge or experience. A payload specialist may fly into space only once.

Shuttle training

The center for astronaut training in the United States is the Johnson Space Center at Houston, Texas. Mission Control, which takes charge of all shuttle missions after lift-off, is also located there. The Russian training base has similar facilities. Known as the Yuri Gagarin Cosmonaut Training Center, it is located at Star City, (Zvezdniy Gorodok) near Moscow.

Pilot-astronauts fly regularly in the shuttle training aircraft. It is equipped with special air brakes so that it can glide at a steep angle, like the shuttle orbiter docs when it comes in to land.

The full-time astronauts undergo lengthy training. They study all aspects of space flight, including navigation and astronomy. Pilot-astronauts fly regularly in high-speed jet planes. Mission specialists practice operating all kinds of shuttle equipment, from the galley (kitchen) unit to the robot arm in the payload bay.

Like the real thing

Astronauts spend much of their time training with full-size mock-ups of the hardware they will be handling in space. For example, they train in mock-ups of the flight deck, mid-deck, payload bay, and other parts of the shuttle orbiter.

The mock-ups are equipped in every way like the real thing. As they practice, the astronauts become familiar with the layout of instruments and controls and the operations they will have to carry out in space.

Mission Simulators

Above: **A shuttle crew trains in a realistic mock-up of the flight deck of the shuttle orbiter. Like most shuttle training facilities, this mock-up is located at the Johnson Space Center, Houston.**

The most realistic mock-ups used in astronaut training are the machines called simulators. Their instruments and controls are "live" and behave in exactly the same way as they would on a real mission. They work through a computer that is programmed to react in a realistic way.

In the most advanced simulators, the computer projects an image on to a screen. This shows the kind of view an astronaut would see out of the window of his or her spacecraft. As the astronaut works the controls, the view changes as it would in real life.

The most realistic simulations take place shortly before the astronauts are due to lift off. The simulators are linked to Mission Control, and the crew and Mission Control rehearse the upcoming mission in every detail.

Space Camp

If you think you would like to become an astronaut, your first step might be to go to Florida's Space Camp, located near the Kennedy Space Center. At the camp you will ride in machines like the multi-axis trainer (right), which twirls you around in all directions. You will help design new space structures, and fly missions in a dummy space shuttle. You will tour Kennedy Spaceport and see historic rockets like the mammoth Saturn V. You will also take a trip out to the launch pads and may be lucky enough to see the spectacular lift-off of a space shuttle. You may even bump into one of the real astronauts.

Above: **Astronauts pose on the mid-deck of the shuttle orbiter for the traditional in-flight photo. The question is: who is right side up and who is upside-down? There is no answer to the question, because in the weightless world of space, there is no up or down.**

Living in Space

Getting into space and living in the space environment presents human beings with many problems. We are used to living in an atmosphere of air and under the gentle tug of Earth's gravity. Providing living quarters in space with an artificial atmosphere is not a difficult problem (see page 134). There are problems in human space flight, however, relating to gravity and other forces that act on the human body.

Getting into space requires astronauts to ride in a rocket-propelled craft that accelerates them at a terrifying rate. It creates forces several times stronger than gravity. We call them g-forces. You experience mild g-forces in a car when the driver accelerates rapidly. You feel yourself pinned to your seat. When astronauts rocket into space, they experience much higher g-forces, which make their bodies feel many times heavier than usual.

Yet when they get into orbit around the Earth, they feel as if their bodies have no weight at all. This peculiar state in orbit is called weightlessness, or zero-g.

A Weightless World

Astronauts feel weightless in orbit. It appears as if gravity has disappeared, but it hasn't. The Earth is still tugging at their bodies, making them fall, but they are traveling so fast around the Earth in orbit that the amount they fall equals the amount the ground curves away beneath them. In effect, they stay the same height above the Earth as human satellites (see page 85).

Space scientists refer to the state of weightlessness as free fall, because astronauts in orbit are in effect falling around the Earth.

Day-to-day living

Weightlessness dominates life in orbit. It affects the way you move, drink, eat, sleep, wash, and even how you go to the toilet. You can't walk around like you

Right: **Pilot-astronaut Michael Baker takes a bite at a passing sandwich on the flight deck of shuttle orbiter Atlantis. Unorthodox eating methods are possible in the strange world of weightlessness.**

Right inset: **America's first woman in space, Sally Ride, enjoys a well-earned sleep during her first flight into space in June 1983. She is sleeping zipped into a sleeping bag anchored to a bunk, or sleep station, on the mid-deck of the shuttle orbiter.**

can on Earth, because there is nothing to keep your feet on the floor. If you press your feet against something, you simply bounce off. If you bend down to pick up something, you start turning somersaults.

You can't drink normally either. If you tried to pour yourself a glass of cola, the liquid would stay in the bottle. You have to suck up liquids through a straw. Sucking only requires air pressure to work, and your spacecraft cabin is pressurized with air to keep you alive.

The flushing toilet

Going to the toilet in space also presents a problem. You need something to remove urine and solid waste as they leave the body. Otherwise they would just float around.

On the space shuttle, there is a regular toilet with a flushing mechanism to remove wastes. Instead of being flushed with a stream of water like a toilet on Earth, it is flushed with a stream of air.

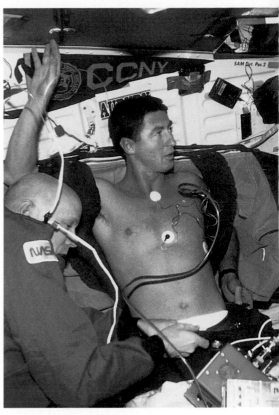

Above: **On every space mission, astronauts carry out experiments to investigate the effects of space flight on the human body. Here Story Musgrave (left) is helping Tom Henricks with an experiment on the circulation of the blood.**

Left: **One of the main jobs of the shuttle mission specialists is to launch spacecraft. Here a communications satellite, is sent spinning into space from a protective pod in the payload bay.**

Life Support

On Earth we are kept alive and protected by an atmosphere of air. It gives us oxygen to breathe and exerts pressure on our bodies. In space there is neither air, oxygen, nor pressure. Therefore, when we venture into space we must take an artificial atmosphere with us.

On a spacecraft the atmosphere is provided by the life support system. This system provides artificial air and keeps it fresh by removing the carbon dioxide you give out when you breathe. The system also keeps the air at a comfortable temperature and humidity. It works in much the same way as a home air conditioner.

Shuttle astronaut Bruce McCandless wriggles out of his spacesuit trousers. He is wearing an undergarment with built-in tubing. When he was spacewalking, water would be circulated through the tubing to keep him cool.

Spacewalking

Sometimes astronauts have to leave their spacecraft to work outside in space. This activity is known popularly as spacewalking. Space scientists call it EVA – extravehicular activity.

When astronauts go spacewalking, they wear a special suit to protect them from the hostile space environment. The shuttle spacesuit, for example, is made up of many layers and has a built-in backpack. This contains a portable life support system, which supplies the suit with oxygen for breathing, along with water and electricity. The water is circulated through the astronaut's special underwear to prevent the body from overheating.

Through the airlock

Spacewalking astronauts leave and return to their spacecraft by way of an airlock. This is a chamber from which the air can be removed. On the shuttle orbiter, the airlock is located on the mid-deck. It is fitted with two hatches. One leads from the mid-deck and the other opens into the payload bay and space.

The astronauts put on their spacesuits in the airlock. They depressurize, or remove air from the airlock, then they can open the exit hatch and float out into space. After their spacewalk, they re-enter the airlock and close the exit hatch. They can now repressurize the airlock and take off their suits.

Bruce McCandless made space history in February 1984 when he made the first untethered spacewalk. Here he is flying in a jet-propelled backpack called the MMU (manned maneuvering unit). At one point he flew over 300 feet (nearly 100 meters) away from shuttle orbiter Challenger, firing jets of gas from sets of thrusters located around the MMU.

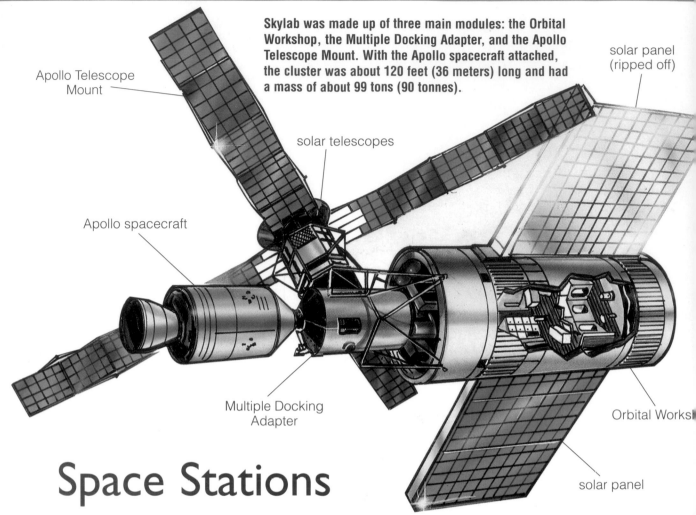

Skylab was made up of three main modules: the Orbital Workshop, the Multiple Docking Adapter, and the Apollo Telescope Mount. With the Apollo spacecraft attached, the cluster was about 120 feet (36 meters) long and had a mass of about 99 tons (90 tonnes).

Apollo Telescope Mount

solar telescopes

solar panel (ripped off)

Apollo spacecraft

Multiple Docking Adapter

Orbital Works

solar panel

Space Stations

In the early days of manned space flight, astronauts spent only a short time in space in cramped spacecraft. They had little time and little room to carry out scientific observations and experiments. However, in April 1971 the Russians launched into orbit a new kind of spacecraft, called Salyut 1. It was bigger than earlier craft and was designed for astronauts to live in for long periods.

Salyut 1 was the world's first space station. Space stations are designed for long stays in space, during which astronauts can carry out valuable long-term observations and experiments.

Six other Salyuts were launched over the next 11 years, each one more successful than the one before. Teams of cosmonauts visited the space stations repeatedly, some remaining in space for months at a time.

The last in the series, Salyut 7, remained in operation until 1986. Then the Russians launched the first

Long Gone

On December 21, 1987, Russian cosmonauts Musakhi Manarov and Vladimir Titov left Earth to fly to the Mir space station. Their feet did not touch the ground again for another 365 days, 22 hours 39 minutes.

module of their present space station-Mir. This module proved to be a base unit, to which other modules were later attached. It contains the living quarters for the station crew, while the other modules are used for observations and experiments.

Sky laboratory

In the United States, NASA designed an experimental space station using hardware left over from the Apollo Moon landing project. Called Skylab, it was made up of three main modules. The largest, the Orbital Workshop, was built around the second stage of a Saturn V rocket. It was a Saturn V rocket that launched Skylab into orbit in May 1973.

Unfortunately, Skylab was badly damaged during the launch, but the first team of three astronauts to visit it was able to carry out repairs and make it habitable. They stayed in Skylab for 28 days. Two further crews were sent – for 59 and 84 days. respectively – smashing all records for lengths of stay in space.

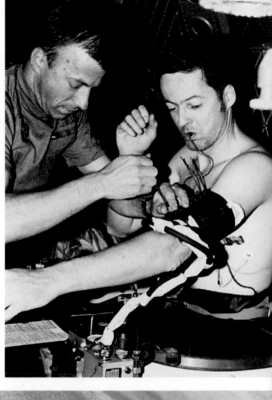

The Skylab crews carried out many successful experiments and observations, particularly of the Sun. They remained remarkably fit during the missions, showing for the first time that human beings could safely live in space for long periods.

Top right: **On the first Skylab mission Paul Weitz (left) assists Dr. Joseph Kerwin in a medical experiment.**

Right: **Skylab in orbit, with a Sunshade fastened over the damaged area of the Orbital Workshop.**

Spacelab goes into space aboard its space shuttle and remains in the payload all the time.

Spacelab

International Cooperation

NASA scientists have been making ambitious plans for another space station for many years. Unfortunately, space budget cuts have forced them to choose a much smaller station than they would like.

The design of the station, is not yet finalized, but it will include a number of modules roughly the size of Spacelab (see box on page 139) linked together. They will be provided by NASA and space agencies in Europe and Japan. Canada and Russia will supply other equipment. The various parts of the station will be carried into orbit by space shuttles and assembled there.

Space medicine

All long-term space missions devote a lot of time to space medicine. This is the study of how the human body is affected by the space environment and how it can be protected

Below: **This is one of many designs that have been proposed over the years for the international space station. It will be built by NASA, with major contributions from Europe, Japan, Canada, and Russia.**

from suffering lasting harm.

The state of weightlessness causes most of the problems. At least 30 percent of the astronauts suffer from space sickness for the first few days in orbit. Space scientists call this condition space adaptation syndrome. It is a form of travel sickness, caused by the balance organs in the ears becoming confused.

More seriously, the muscles of the body begin to waste away because there is no gravity to fight against. The muscles of the heart are affected too, which upsets the blood circulation. Another worrying effect of long space flights is a loss of bone tissue.

However, most of these harmful effects can be combatted. Regular exercise on machines such as treadmills and exercise bikes helps keep the muscles toned up, and a special diet helps to fight the loss of bone tissue. As a result, human beings can remain in space for months at a time without suffering permanent damage to their bodies.

Looking ahead

This bodes well for the long-term future of space exploration. In the 21st century, astronauts are expected to return to the Moon and set up permanent bases there. Later they will take a mighty leap into the unknown and head for the planet Mars. This is the only planet on which conditions are suitable for human beings to explore.

Right: **Regular experiments on Spacelab missions investigate the causes of space sickness. Here payload specialist Millie Hughes-Fulford is helping James Bagian in an experiment with a rotating chair device.**

Europe's Space Laboratory

Much valuable space science is carried out in Spacelab, a fully equipped space laboratory built by the European Space Agency. It is carried into space by its space shuttle, and remains inside the payload bay all the time.

Spacelab is a model for the kind of laboratory units that will form an essential part of the international space station. The main part of Spacelab is the pressurized laboratory module, in which scientists work. On some missions, extra instruments are flown on a platform, or pallet, open to space.

Spacelab investigators carry out research in many branches of science. They conduct experiments in biology and medicine, materials science, astronomy, and space physics. They also take photographs of the Earth and observe the heavens through telescopes. Some Spacelab missions are devoted entirely to the study of the life sciences. Scientists investigate how the space environment affects animal and plant life and humans.

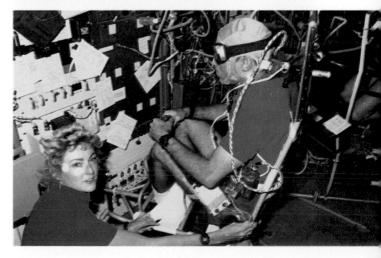

Glossary

airlock A chamber in a spacecraft from which the air can be removed. Astronauts pass through an airlock before they go spacewalking.

asteroids Small rocky bodies that orbit the Sun between the orbits of Mars and Jupiter. They are also called minor planets.

astronomy The scientific study of the heavens.

aurora A glow seen in the sky, mostly in the polar regions. It is caused by charged particles from outer space interacting with air molecules.

Big Bang An event that is thought to have happened about 15 billion years ago and to have created the Universe.

black hole An incredibly dense body with such enormous gravity that nothing, not even light, can escape from its clutches.

booster The first stage of a launch vehicle, or an additional stage added to it to provide extra power at lift-off.

celestial sphere An imaginary sphere surrounding the Earth, to which the stars seem to be attached.

comet A heavenly body that starts to shine when it comes near the Sun. It is a large lump of rock, ice, and dust.

communications satellite A satellite used to relay radio and other communications signals from country to country.

constellation A pattern that can be seen in the night sky, made by a number of bright stars.

cosmic rays Streams of electrically charged particles that bombard the Earth from outer space.

countdown The counting down of a period of time before a launch vehicle lifts off.

crater A hole in the surface of a planet or Moon, usually made by a meteorite.

docking The joining up of two craft in space.

eclipse The passing of one heavenly body across the face of another, so that it appears to blot out its light. During a solar eclipse, the Moon blots out the Sun's light. During a lunar eclipse, the Moon moves into the Earth's shadow.

ecliptic The path the Sun appears to follow each year around the celestial sphere.

encounter A meeting in space between a space probe and a heavenly body.

equinoxes Times of the year when the lengths of day and night are equal. This happens when the Sun crosses the celestial equator – on March 21 (vernal, or spring equinox) and on September 23 (autumnal equinox).

escape velocity The speed a spacecraft must have to escape from Earth's gravity.

EVA Abbreviation for extravehicular activity, meaning activity outside a spacecraft. It is usually called spacewalking.

fuel cell A cell used to power spacecraft, including the space shuttle. It produces electricity by combining hydrogen with oxygen, forming water.

galaxy A star island in space. Our galaxy is called the Milky Way.

geostationary orbit An orbit 22,300 miles (35,900 km) high above the Equator. In this orbit a satellite takes 24 hours to circle the Earth.

g-forces Gravitational forces produced when a rocket or a spacecraft accelerates rapidly.

gravity The pull of the Earth on anything on it or near it in space. A similar force exists between any two bodies anywhere in the Universe.

heat shield An outer covering on a spacecraft, designed to protect it from the heat of re-entry into the atmosphere.

interstellar matter A mixture of gas and dust found in tiny amounts throughout outer space.

launch vehicle A combination of rockets built to launch spacecraft.

life-support system A spacecraft system that provides suitable conditions for a human crew to live in space.

light-year A common unit astronomers use to measure distances in space. It is the distance light travels in a year – some 5.9 million million miles (9.5 million million km).

magnitude A scale on which star brightness is measured. The brightest stars visible to the naked eye are rated 1st magnitude; those just barely visible to the naked eye are rated 6th magnitude.

mare (plural, maria) A plains region on the Moon. *Mare* is the Latin word for "sea."

meteor A piece of rock from outer space that creates a streak of light as it burns up in the atmosphere.

meteorite A piece of rock from outer space that survives to reach the ground.

Milky Way A glowing band visible in the night sky on a really dark night. It is also the name of our galaxy.

mission control A control center for a space mission, such as Mission Control at Houston, Texas, which controls shuttle flights.

NASA Abbreviation for the National Aeronautics and Space Administration, the organization that coordinates space activities in the United States.

nebula A bright or dark cloud of gas and dust found in the space between the stars.

neutron star An incredibly dense star made up of neutrons.

nova A star that suddenly flares up and increases dramatically in brightness.

nuclear fusion A process that produces the energy that keeps the stars shining. It involves the fusion (coming together) of the nuclei (centers) of hydrogen atoms.

orbit A path in space taken by any small body circling around a larger one and bound to it by gravity, such as the Earth's path around the Sun, or an artificial satellite's path around the Earth.

orbital velocity The speed a spacecraft needs to remain in orbit around the Earth. At a height of 200 miles (300 km), the orbital velocity is about 17,500 mph (28,000 km/h).

payload The cargo a launch vehicle carries, such as a satellite.

phases The different shapes of the Moon we see during the month as more or less of it is lit up by the Sun.

planet A large body that circles around the Sun. The Earth is one of nine planets in our Solar System.

probe A spacecraft that escapes from Earth's gravity and travels to other heavenly bodies.

propellant A substance burned in a rocket to produce the gases that propel it.

pulsar A neutron star that spins rapidly and gives off rapid pulses of radiation.

quasar A heavenly body that looks like a star but lies much farther away. It gives off the energy of hundreds of galaxies.

radio astronomy A branch of astronomy that studies the radio waves heavenly bodies give out.

red giant A large red star, formed when a much smaller star grows old and expands.

remote sensing Collecting information about the Earth's surface from orbiting satellites.

rocket An engine used to power launch vehicles. It burns fuel to produce a stream of hot gases. As these gases shoot out backward from the motor, a force (thrust) is set up that propels the motor forward.

RTG Abbreviation for radioisotope thermoelectric generator. This device converts heat given off by a radioactive substance into electricity.

solar cell A cell that converts solar energy into electricity.

solar system The family of the Sun. It includes the planets and their Moons, the asteroids, meteors, and comets.

solar wind A stream of charged particles given off by the Sun.

spacewalking The popular term for extravehicular activity, or EVA.

star A huge globe of searing hot gas, which produces energy as light, heat, and other radiation.

supergiant A very large star, with more than a hundred times the diameter of the Sun.

telescope The main instrument astronomers use to look at the stars. Refractors use lenses, and reflectors use mirrors to gather and focus the light from the stars.

tracking Keeping track of a spacecraft as it travels through space.

trajectory The path a spacecraft follows through space.

UFO Abbreviation for unidentified flying object. Some people believe that UFOs are craft sent by an alien civilization.

Universe Everything that exists, including the Earth, Moon, Sun, stars, galaxies, and even space itself.

weightlessness The peculiar state that exists in orbit, in which nothing seems to have any weight. Another term for this state is free fall.

white dwarf A very dense small star, near the end of its life.

zodiac A band of the celestial sphere through which the Sun, Moon, and planets appear to move. It passes through 12 constellations – the constellations of the zodiac.

Index